# BEASTLY LAW

**Fenton Bresler** has successfully combined the roles of barrister, journalist and author for more than thirty years. As Legal Correspondent of the *Sunday Express* he contributes a weekly column on the law – 'What Is Your Verdict?' – as well as regular series on murder investigation and other major crime. Among the books he has written is the official biography of the former Lord Chief Justice Goddard; *The Trail of the Triads*, an international investigation into the world's most sinister crime organisation; *Second Best Bed*, a diversion on wills; and a highly acclaimed biography of the writer Georges Simenon. He has written for both television and radio, and frequently appears on programmes dealing with crime and other aspects of the law.

Fenton Bresler

# BEASTLY LAW

Illustrated by Nicola Jennings

## A GRAHAM TARRANT BOOK

### DAVID & CHARLES

Newton Abbot   London   North Pomfret (Vt)

British Library Cataloguing in Publication Data

Bresler, Fenton
    Beastly law.——(A Graham Tarrant book)
    1. Animals, Treatment of——Law and
    legislation
    I. Title
    342.647      K3620

    ISBN 0–7153–8828–2

Typeset by Photo-graphics, Honiton, Devon
and printed in Great Britain
by A. Wheaton & Co Ltd, Hennock Road, Exeter
for David & Charles Publishers plc
Brunel House    Newton Abbot    Devon

Published in the United States of America
by David & Charles Inc
North Pomfret    Vermont 05053    USA

*To Timmy*
*our cat*

*Senator Incitatus Equus*

# PAMPERED PETS

Caligula was only one Roman emperor who thought more of animals than of human beings. He made his horse, Incitatus, a senator. The Emperor Nero, perhaps the most evil of that group of men, awarded pensions to his retired racehorses, which were dressed in human clothing for the presentation ceremonies.

In Imperial China, Royal Pekinese puppies were suckled by human wet nurses specially trained for the task. While back in ancient Rome, the poet Virgil spent the equivalent of £50,000 on the funeral of his favourite pet fly. There was, however, in his case perhaps another reason for his generosity. He declared the burial area a cemetery, which enabled him to avoid payment of a land tax.

In modern Rome, two Italian journalists let their concern for their seal land them in trouble with the law. In 1951 they were fined for letting him have a swim in the waters of the Trevi Fountain, in breach of a regulation which says the only thing which can be thrown into the fountain is money.

In November 1985, a German double-killer, Herbert Solf, who had almost completed a life sentence for murdering two women, was allowed out of jail for a day to look for a job. He failed to return. While a full-scale hunt was launched, the prison governor at Fuhlbttel jail, near Hamburg, told the press: 'Solf has left behind his two cats. If he does not come back, we will have to have them put to sleep.'

Hardly had the interview been published than Solf rang the prison promising to give himself up. As good as his word, he reported back to jail a few hours later. 'Those cats have helped me through the most difficult years of my life,' he said. 'I could not be so heartless as to let them die.'

# PARTNERS IN CRIME

Sometimes there is a practical value to making a good friend of your pet – and not only a dog. In 1930, there was a spate of burglaries in Chicago which had the police puzzled, until they realised that burglars were training monkeys to squeeze through the narrowest skylights and other small apertures to open doors for their masters from within.

The detectives realised what they were up against when, on investigating a jewel robbery, they found that someone must have got into the flat through a ventilator too narrow to admit even the body of a small boy. But then they discovered the prints of a monkey's paws on the paint around the ventilator, and there were similar tracks on the floor of the flat leading to the back door. All the animal had needed to do was unlock the door from the inside and let in his criminally-minded owner.

In Czechoslovakia in the mid-1930s, two travelling fair-men discovered that a certain concoction of herbs gave off a pungent smell that infuriated a performing bear. They knew that a wealthy local recluse was in the habit of walking along a particularly lonely road on his way home. So they hid in the trees with the bear, and when they saw the man coming, put the herbal concoction under the animal's nostrils – and jumped smartly back. The bear promptly mauled the old man to death, whereupon the two villains robbed him.

As with so many murderers, their vanity led to their undoing. When drunk, they boasted about how clever they had been – and the police got the message!

In India, 'snakebite' is a traditional way of disposing of those you want to get rid of, one of its attractions being that it is almost impossible to trace the real killer. Sometimes a cobra is inserted into a hollow bamboo, which is then laid down beside the sleeping victim. The reptile, which has been irritated, is then allowed to escape and takes its revenge upon the first person it sees: the innocent sleeper.

Suicides, too, have used animals and insects. One Steven Liarski, in New York, decided to kill himself. He read that the bite of a Black Widow spider was deadly, and that there was no known cure. So he purchased one of these spiders from California. It worked. After Liarski had allowed the spider to bite him, the insect was found in a perforated cardboard box carefully placed beside the dead man's bed.

Even in rural Britain animal accomplices in crime have been known. When in the early 1930s, following a spate of thefts, the Worcester Golf Club professional put eighteen marked balls down on the course, with a policeman hidden nearby, it was a human thief they were expecting to catch. But a dog came along, picked up a ball and took it straight to its fifty-two-year-old master, who patted it on the back and put the ball in his pocket. Needless to say, it was the man not the dog who was arrested and subsequently fined.

Not every animal in the service of crime succeeds. In 1985, an alsatian dog called Rebel turned out to be his master's worst friend when he helped police solve a £5,500 burglary. The dog was caught at the scene of the crime in Highgate, London – and then led police officers through one and a half miles of North London roads to his home in Kentish Town, where lived his nineteen-year-old owner.

As well as making the mistake of taking his dog with him to the burglary, the young man also chose the wrong date to commit his offence: Friday, the 13th.

# HOUSE GUESTS

A horse-loving young woman in Chelmsford, Essex, used to buy unwanted horses to save them from the knacker's yard. That was an entirely worthy mission, but she had her problems as she later explained: 'I used to keep them in a field in the country, but people kept letting them out! Then the snow came and I felt sorry for them because they were so cold. I had bought a house three months ago to restore and it seemed an ideal place to keep the horses for the winter.'

So what she did was to install in this pleasant, detached house in a charming residential road in Chelmsford, a stallion named Dougal and his three equine friends. They had a dining-room, lounge, fitted kitchen and bathroom to themselves.

But the neighbours kicked at this. They complained that the clatter of hooves in the small hours gave them nightmares. One eighty-two-year-old lady said: 'It's terrible. I've lived forty-two years in this area and it used to be a respectable neighbourhood. Now it's like living in a zoo. Since the horses moved in next door all we get is banging and snorting at all hours of the night and the smell of rotting hay. They have smashed up the house and turned the garden into a quagmire. It's a bit of a shock to wake up in the morning and see a fully grown horse peering at you from the bedroom window across the way.'

In vain, the young woman protested that her horses were very well behaved and did not smell at all. In February 1982, the local Council used its legal powers to order her to remove her house guests immediately.

# MORE MONKEY BUSINESS

In the early 1930s, two performing monkeys died at the hands of a firing squad in the courtyard of Cairo Central Prison. They were the pets of an Egyptian named Abdul Said, who had been arrested for distracting a woman's attention by making the monkeys do tricks while he stole a £20 bracelet from her wrist.

When the animals were taken to the police station, they put up such a fierce resistance to the officers, biting them and tearing up the police furniture, that they had to be chained and put in prison themselves. In desperation, the police turned to the authorities at the Cairo Zoo. But they, too, found they could do nothing with the two fractious prisoners.

As nobody could be found to look after them, it was decided that the monkeys must die. They were given a meal treated with arsenic. But not only did the animals refuse to eat it, they went on hunger strike and would eat nothing. In the end, to stop them dying of hunger, the prison authorities had them face the firing squad.

# DEATH AT THE OLD BAILEY

Even the world's most famous criminal court has passed sentence of death upon an animal – and in recent times.

In 1952, the formidable Mr Justice Hilbery was presiding in No 2 Court over the trial of a middle-aged labourer charged with strangling his girlfriend. The defendant was sitting quietly in the dock. A woman was in the witness box telling how she had seen the couple struggling in a dark alley, and the jury were paying close attention to the grim tale.

Suddenly a rat appeared in court. Drains were being repaired in the basement following war damage, and the rat had somehow got into the ventilating system and had clambered out through a grille. It scuffled into a corner where it stayed motionless. A reporter, sitting in the press box in front of the jury, pointed towards the animal and mouthed the word 'rat' to the clerk of the court.

Two women jurors stifled their screams. The barristers turned in their seats, and defence counsel cross-examining the witness stopped in mid-question. The witness also stifled a scream. Even the prisoner, on trial for his life, stood up and leaned over the ledge of the dock looking at the frightened animal cowering a few feet away from him. Mr Justice Hilbery, ice-cold as ever, was equal to the occasion. In calm, unhurried tones, he said: 'I will adjourn the court for ten minutes' – and added: 'Perhaps when the rat is caught, it will be expeditiously executed.'

As soon as, with black cap in hand, he had left the court, the first man to reach the rat was the prison doctor, who always had to attend a murder trial at that time. But he did nothing. He merely looked at the creature and quietly returned to his seat. Afterwards he explained: 'I just wanted to see what colour it was, grey or black. Bubonic plague, you know.'

Others were more resolute. Ushers and police officers closed in on the animal and it was taken into custody. Down in the basement it was 'expeditiously executed', and upstairs the trial was resumed – which ended in the man in the dock suffering the same fate.

*Three months of retreat for bad language*

# ANIMALS IN THE DOCK

In the Middle Ages, it was not only humans who were put on trial for criminal offences. It was not unknown for it to happen to animals as well. The alleged basis for this was Mosaic Law, according to which (Exodus xxi 28), 'If an ox gore a man or a woman, that they die, the ox shall be surely stoned ... but the owner of the ox shall be quit.'

Domestic animals were tried in the ordinary civil courts, but proceedings against wild animals were taken in ecclesiastical courts – where the penalty was exorcising, anathematising and excommunicating. Thus, there is the well authenticated case of the nuns of a convent at Nevers several centuries later who condemned their parrot to two months of abstinence, three of retreat and four of silence as a punishment for using bad language which it had picked up on a voyage by water to Nantes.

The domestic animals facing trial in the civil courts were in much greater peril than their wild brothers, for they were often formally convicted of a capital crime, taken out and executed.

In 1474 in Basle, Switzerland, a cock was tried on the charge of laying an egg. Despite the valiant efforts of defence counsel who claimed that laying an egg was an involuntary act and therefore not punishable in law, the cock was found guilty and, together with his egg, burnt at the stake – 'not as a cock but as a sorcerer or devil in the form of a cock.' Modern scientific opinion takes more the view that the poor creature was, in fact, genuinely an old hen which sometimes do assume cocks' plumage.

Seventeen years previously, in 1457, at Lavegny in France, a sow and her six young piglets were charged with having murdered and partly eaten a child. After a solemn trial, the sow was found guilty and executed; but the piglets were acquitted on account of their youth, the bad example of their mother, and the absence of direct proof as to whether they had been able to get a look in when their mother was busy guzzling the child.

At Anton, Switzerland, a large family of rats were the defendants. They were described in the official records of the courts as 'dirty animals in the form of rats, of a greyish colour, living in holes.' The rodents ignored the summons, but were so ably defended by counsel that the court did not insist upon their appearance.

At Selveio in Northern Italy in 1519, the local field mice were convicted of having caused damage to food crops. The sentence of the court was banishment for life, and in order to make sure that the order was complied with, they were given safe conduct into exile with an escorted trip out of town and all cats kept locked away.

Even so docile an animal as a cow was, in 1740, sentenced to be executed by a French court for attacking a little girl. The judge himself was present when the sentence was carried out, for which the condemned animal was dressed in doublet, stockings, gloves and lace cuffs.

Sometimes, however, mercy was shown. Sentences *could* be commuted. In 1379, Philip the Bold, Duke of Burgundy, reprieved and pardoned two herds of swine which had been condemned to death as accomplices of three sows found guilty of infanticide. And in 1750, in France, a she-ass which had been condemned to death was pardoned because of her former good character.

# TRIAL BY BATTLE

Fighting it out between accuser and suspect to see who was really guilty of a crime continued effective in English law until the early nineteenth century. In the last recorded case, Thornton *v* Ashford, in 1817, Thornton was accused of murdering Mary Ashford. Thornton claimed the right to challenge his accuser, Mary's brother, to Trial by Battle.

Such a claim had not been made for well over 200 years, but Lord Ellenborough, the Lord Chief Justice (whose other main entitlement to fame is his remark that transportation was 'merely a transfer to a more salubrious climate'), ruled that Trial by Battle was still available. He allowed the suit, but Mary's brother refused to accept Thornton's challenge – and Thornton was at once set free. We will never know whether or not he was guilty, but two years later Parliament decided it had had enough of this medieval practice and finally abolished Trial by Battle in English law.

No animal has ever figured in Trial by Battle in an English court. Not so in France. It happened in Paris on 8 August 1361 before the King, John II.

A Monsieur de Montdidier had been murdered while travelling through the forest of Bondy, and buried beneath a tree. His dog eventually came scratching at a friend's door and led him to the grave.

Some time afterwards the dog, usually well-behaved, flew at a man's throat and almost killed him. Suspicions were aroused, and word reached the King. He had the dog and the man called before him, and saw for himself the way in which the dog had to be restrained from attacking the man. He decided that man and dog should fight it out, and that God should give his verdict.

So it was done. The man was armed with a stick and the dog provided with a wooden box into which he could retreat. A space was cleared on a specially erected stage in front of Notre Dame, and the fight began. The dog won and the man, held again by the throat, confessed to the crime.

# FAGIN'S KENNEL

It is not only small children that can be taught to steal. Animals can also be willing students. One such creature was Yarrow, a sheep dog that was just too clever for its own good.

Yarrow's master used to walk through his neighbours' flocks with the dog by his side, under pretence of selecting sheep to purchase. At the same time, he would give a well-understood signal to the dog, which would go largely unnoticed by anyone else. Then at night Yarrow would return to the flock and bring away the sheep that his master had indicated, sometimes as many as a dozen.

Yarrow was amazing. He would unerringly single out the designated animals from a large flock and, detaching them from their comrades, drive them for several miles by a circuitous route to the hiding place where his master was waiting to receive them. Sadly, sheepstealing was, in the eighteenth century, such a pest for law-abiding farmers that, when caught, both master and dog were executed.

In more recent times, in Paris, in 1922, a butcher in the rue St Charles was annoyed by a dog that every morning visited his shop and carried off a joint of meat. This happened so regularly that the butcher became suspicious, and had the dog followed. At a rendezvous point nearby, a woman was seen to take the meat from the dog's mouth. She was promptly arrested for training the dog to steal for her.

# A NICE LEGAL POINT

Sir Walter Scott tells an interesting tale about a cow, happening to pass along a road, that drank up a tub of home-brewed ale which a Forfarshire housewife had set outside her door to cool. The cow was admittedly 'the worse for drink', but the question was: ought her owner to pay for the ale? In the event he refused, and was duly summoned by the housewife before the local bailie.

This learned judge asked whether the cow had taken her refreshment standing or sitting. It was at once admitted that the cow had been standing. The bailie then 'solemnly adjudged the cow's drink to be *deoch an dornis.*' This meant that it was a stirrup cup, or a parting drink, traditionally given to travellers at the start of a journey, for which no charge could be made without violating the ancient hospitality of Scotland.

# BEWARE OF THE LION!

'Beware of the Lion' said the sign on the gate of a suburban garden in Worcestershire in 1975, but a young man calling in search of work thought it was a joke. So getting no reply from a knock at the front door, and seeing a light on at the rear of the house, he clambered over the seven-foot-high back garden fence. 'Suddenly something leapt out of the dark onto my back and completely floored me,' he later told the police. 'I suddenly realised, "Good God, it *is* a lion!"' One-year-old Laddo had been bought by the houseowner a year earlier as a protection after two burglaries.

But English law had not been broken. A police spokesman explained: 'We have interviewed the houseowner and we are not happy with the situation. But the caller was legally a trespasser and the lion was not loose, so there is no question of any prosecution.'

The answer would be different today: in the following year, Parliament passed the 1976 Dangerous Wild Animals Act which states that anyone keeping a wild animal, as a pet or a protection, must first obtain a licence from his local authority. And a licence will only be granted if veterinary inspectors are satisfied that the animal is kept in suitable escape-proof accommodation and – most important – properly fed.

Yet there still is no power in English law to order a man to destroy his dangerous lion. Not so with dangerous dogs. They *can* be 'put down' by decree of a court, and you cannot always count on a Bench being as understanding as the Gloucester magistrates who, when a defendant admitted before them that his dog was dangerous but added 'I've given it to my mother-in-law', decided not to proceed any further with the case.

In both English and American law, 'every dog is entitled to one bite'. But in one case in Britain in October 1975 this was even extended to one shoot, when a Yorkshireman out with his red setter on the Moors at Errington, near Halifax, was shot – accidentally, of course – by his own dog. He put his gun against the wall as he climbed over and the animal, scrambling up with him, caught the trigger with its paw.

No doubt if he had done it deliberately, his owner recovering in hospital might have been minded to get a destruction order from the nearest magistrates' court. But they are not easy to obtain in this country of dog lovers.

'He is my only witness, my Lord,' said counsel some years ago at the Inner London Sessions Appeals Committee when a handsome labrador named Rover walked amiably into court, tail wagging, tongue lolling. The Committee chairman stood up and looked Rover over. A Committee member called his name and a friendly tail wagged furiously. All hearts melted – and the Old Street magistrate's order that Rover, a local publican's pet, should be destroyed was quashed. After all, he had only bitten two elderly women.

Nothing seems able to deter a judge resolute not to be beastly to beasts. In December 1975 Dashtanga Golden Winthrop, a twelve-stone Great Dane called 'Caliph' by his many friends, was doomed to be destroyed by order of the Bedfordshire magistrates. Only one hand could stay the deadly edict – that of Judge Robert Lymbery, QC at Bedford Crown Court.

So what happened? Caliph promptly bit that hand when the judge, after patting him on the head, tried to examine his teeth. Returned to court, with a handkerchief wrapped around his bleeding limb, His Honour announced his decision and that of the two magistrates sitting with him: 'With a certain amount of anxiety,' they were quashing the destruction order. 'What I did was my own fault, which is why I am not complaining,' explained Judge Lymbery with charming gallantry.

But then he was only echoing the sentiment expressed by Judge Hugh Mais (later elevated to the High Court as Mr Justice Mais) some time earlier in the West London County Court, when a barrister had commented before him, 'a dog is a mindless creature'. 'I do not think you will receive any sympathy from dog lovers when you make a statement like that,' sternly reproved the judge.

They are not so cosy about canines in Libya. When, in 1974, a dog was put on trial in Tripoli on the charge of biting a human, he was duly convicted and sentenced to a month in jail on bread and water.

# THE DOCTOR AND THE CAT

Britain is justly proud of the fact that rabies stops at Calais, but the price is strict anti-rabies laws.

Until 1974, the only penalty for smuggling animals into the country was a fine, with the result that far too many people were prepared to risk a purely financial penalty for bringing in their pets illegally. So in that year the government brought out a new Rabies Order, whose Article 17 created an indictable offence punishable with an unlimited fine and up to one year in jail for those who deliberately tried to evade the law. But pet smuggling still went on and four years later a forty-five-year-old doctor, returning from South Africa, nearly went to jail because of his wife's love for a cat.

It was really rather a sad story. The doctor's wife was seriously ill. So, on the day after returning to Britain, he paid £5 for a black and white cat that looked just like their own pet Biba, in quarantine at Faringdon in Hampshire, and somehow managed to swop the two animals over.

He was only found out when the substitute cat gave birth in quarantine to kittens, although records showed that the real Biba had been spayed and all the tom cats in the kennels were known to have been neutered. The kennel staff also remembered that Biba hated chicken mince, while this new cat they now had loved it.

Result: the doctor stood in the dock at Winchester Crown Court charged with contravening the 1974 Rabies Order. 'People must be made to realise that these regulations are designed to prevent what would be a terrible disaster to this country if a rabid animal ever got in,' the Recorder told him. He sentenced him to a three months' suspended jail sentence, and fined him £1,000 plus the same again for costs.

# BIRD DROPPINGS

All efforts to recapture four pet canaries failed after vandals broke the door to a school aviary in Bridlington, Humberside, in September 1985. Until, that is, the caretaker called on the police for help.

They had just the man for the job: a police constable who, in his own words, 'knew just what to do. I used to keep pigeons and chickens.' On arrival at the school he asked the caretaker for a garden sieve, some string and a short stick. He then tied the string to the stick, which he used to prop up the edge of the sieve. Next he spread millet around and under the sieve before winding his ball of string out to a safe distance.

Within half an hour the first canary flew down to follow the trail of millet, and eventually hopped under the sieve. The policeman yanked on the string and down came the sieve trapping the bird. He gently returned the bird to the aviary before resetting his makeshift trap. Within two hours all the canaries were safely back in their cage.

The name of the resourceful policeman: PC 'Dickie' Bird.

A canary was in another matter with which the police were concerned some two months earlier. But this time it was in Scotland, and the whole thing ended up in court.

A sixteen-year-old bird fancier and his friend thought they were safe in marching down the street at midnight with nineteen stolen budgerigars, two zebra finches and a canary stuffed inside their clothes. However, loud chirpings from within gave the game away; a policeman with acute hearing came strolling over, and the youth was duly fined £40 for theft.

*Manna from heaven*

It was the lowly pigeon that made legal history in the High Court in London in November 1984, when Judge Raymond Kidwell, QC awarded a sixty-four-year-old spinster £5,866 damages plus interest against the Royal Borough of Kensington and Chelsea for their 'persistent and culpable' failure to clean up pigeon droppings.

The Council had denied liability, but his Lordship ruled that, although the pavement underneath the railway bridge at Latimer Road Underground Station was swept every day, this was not effective to clean up the droppings – described by one witness as 'a white filthy mess'. Between 100 and 200 pigeons used the bridge to roost, with about a dozen roosting directly over the pavement. Overnight these twelve birds would excrete a total of fifty to sixty droppings.

'If the pavement had been given a good sluice with a bucket of water, the danger would have been reduced,' said the judge. But Council workers had not been provided 'with the necessary equipment'.

Judge Kidwell stressed that his decision related to 'this one particular bridge and to this particular local authority.' Even so, an important legal principle of value to the general public had been authoritatively pronounced. In future, pigeon droppings may, in certain circumstances, prove to be manna from heaven.

# ANIMAL SMUGGLERS

As might be expected, cats and dogs are the animals most frequently tried to be smuggled into Britain – at least, they are the ones most often caught. But the range of temptation for pet lovers is remarkably wide.

A policeman at Harwich in Essex was suspicious, in August 1981, when he saw a Dutch girl, newly arrived on a ferry from Holland, nervously fingering her collar. When he and Customs officers searched her, a nineteen-year-old student, they found a fully grown live rat nestling in a headscarf around her neck.

She was travelling with her twenty-four-year-old boyfriend and told officials that she had rescued the rat from a research laboratory. 'It is my pet. I have cared for it for the past five months and it goes everywhere with me,' she said. But the magistrates were stony of heart and ordered the rat to be destroyed, fining the couple £135 with £15 costs each for contravening the Rabies Order.

Another pet rat to get its mistress into trouble was Ted, brought into Britain by a French student in the summer of 1985. Once safely, so she thought, in London, she took him to a pub. Ted escaped. A customer, in the belief that he was a scavenging English rat, stamped him to death. The student was mortified and tried to commit suicide. She failed – and was fined £400 for bringing Ted illegally into the country.

Guinea pigs, a hamster, a female white rat and even six zebra finches hidden down the trousers of a middle-aged male bird lover have all caused their owners to end up in court, being fined.

In March 1978, it was not a traveller that was fined but a worker at Hull docks who took pity on a South American bear smuggled onto a West German cargo ship, and left to fend for itself on the quay. He took the bear home 'running loose in the car' – only to have his wife order him: 'Get it out of the house!' By then the police, alerted by other motorists, had arrived on the scene and arrested both bear and docker. He was fined £400 and ordered to pay £30 costs. What happened to the bear? It was put in quarantine and eventually handed over to a local zoo.

A serious warning was given to all international air travellers, tempted to allow their pets to answer a call of nature during a stopover on British soil, in a case at Wootton Bassett Magistrates' Court, Wiltshire, in November 1983.

The wife of an American working for Lockheed in the Sudan had 'thumbed a lift' from Atlanta on a Sudanese Air Force aircraft which landed for a brief stopover at Lyneham RAF base. She took her Yorkshire terrier, 'Yorkie', for a two-minute 'walkies' on the runway – and it cost her a £400 fine for breach of the Rabies Order.

# THE WORLD'S RICHEST DOG

When American millionairess, Ella Wendel, died in 1931, she left her entire fortune of $30 million to her pet poodle, Toby. But the unlucky animal never lived to enjoy his inheritance. He was shortly afterwards put down on the order of the executors. The reason given was 'senile decay'.

Senile or not, Toby had had a marvellous existence during Miss Wendel's lifetime. He had his own room in her house and had silk cushions and priceless linen to lie on. Each morning his eccentric mistress brought him breakfast in bed, and a butler was specially employed to wait on him. Perhaps there was method in the executors' madness – with many claimants to the vast estate disputing the animal's inheritance. He was made to sleep in a plain basket in the kitchen of the dark, empty house and to eat his food like any ordinary dog, from a bowl. If he had not been destroyed, Toby would almost certainly have died anyway from a broken heart.

# BEASTLY LAWS

British parliamentary draftsmen are renowned for being able to think of everything, and for covering every possible situation in advance by the wording of their statutes.

The Agriculture (Miscellaneous Provisions) Act of 1943 is a splendid example of this remarkable ability. In Section 17 it specifically provides that the artificial insemination of certain specified animals shall only take place 'under the authority of a licence issued by the Minister'. The animals whose sexual activities are thus officially circumscribed? 'Cattle, sheep, goats, swine, horses, domestic fowls, turkeys, geese and ducks.' All others are free to do what comes naturally.

In Section 15 of the 1911 Protection of Animals Act, the draftsman took on the daunting task of defining a 'domestic animal'. This is the definition:

'Any horse, ass, mule, bull, sheep, pig, goat, dog, cat or fowl, or any other animal of whatsoever kind or species, and whether a quadruped or not, which is tame or which has been or is being sufficiently tamed to serve some purpose for the use of man.'

Could *you* improve on that?

It was this 1911 Act that formed the basis of a fascinating decision by the Queen's Bench Divisional Court in London in June 1980. Some twenty months earlier, the stipendiary magistrate at Cardiff had acquitted two actors of cruelty to a goldfish during the performance of an avant garde play at the city's Chapter Arts Centre. In the final scene of *The Last Temptation*, a bowl containing the goldfish, which had been suspended from the ceiling throughout the performance, was dashed to the floor, the water spilled out and the poor goldfish was left gasping for breath.

There was a great deal of argument as to whether goldfish could feel pain, but the stipendiary magistrate came to no decision on that matter. He threw out the case because he ruled that a goldfish was not a 'captive animal' within the meaning of the 1911 Act, which specifically only applies to 'domestic or captive animals'.

Was the goldfish a 'captive animal'? The RSPCA took the case on Appeal to London. The thoughtful draftsman had defined the term, in Section 15(c), as 'any animal (not being a domestic animal) of whatsoever kind or species and whether a quadruped or not, including any bird, fish or reptile, which is in captivity, or confinement, or which is maimed, pinioned or subjected to an appliance or contrivance for the purpose of hindering or preventing its escape from captivity or confinement.' Lord Justice Donaldson and Mr Justice Kilner Brown had no difficulty in ruling that this goldfish was 'in confinement' in accordance with the meaning of the sub-section. Therefore, it was 'a captive animal' and the two actors could be guilty of an offence. But they still got off scot-free. Lord Justice Donaldson said that it would be 'inappropriate' for the case to be sent back to be heard again because it had taken so long to come up on Appeal.

One should not always complain about what Hamlet called 'the law's delay'.

Another nice point of legal interpretation occurred in August 1985. A teenage girl in Dawlish, Devon, stepped under the shower in her bungalow, turned on the tap – and screamed in horror. For she was sprayed all over by earwigs. Her ninety-three-year-old neighbour also found her bath filled with them. 'They come out of the taps and crawl over towels and flannels,' she told a reporter.

The plague had struck all six bungalows in a little parade in that delightful West Country town. Unfortunately, as the earwigs were 'not a danger to public health' the Council said they did not come within Public Health legislation and it could do nothing about them.

# ALL DOWN TO DRINK

Drinking to excess takes people in the strangest ways. In the summer of 1985, it even made a Parisian businessman, holidaying in Majorca, mistake a lioness for his wife.

It happened in the early morning. His wife was still sleeping in the spare room where she had gone after he had come rolling home at past midnight, when, still hungover, he felt his ear being licked. He thought she had forgiven him and turned over to find himself about to cuddle ... a lioness.

He ran naked into the street and police, who could smell alcohol on his breath, were just about to arrest him as he gabbled his story, when they saw the lioness walk out of his holiday bungalow. So he avoided detention; but the owner of the lioness, which had escaped from a circus, was charged with failing to keep the animal under proper control.

Police in Worthing, Sussex, had the fright of their lives when they stopped a motorist for a breath test late one night and found a ten-foot pet python coiled round his waist. A police sergeant said: 'It was asleep and the driver explained that he took his pet everywhere with him.' The incident had a happy ending. Both man and snake were later released.

A twenty-year-old reveller picked up a penguin after a night's activity, and it cost him £700 at Southport Magistrates' Court in December 1983.

What had happened was that after a night's solid drinking the young man had gone for an early morning stroll to sober up. It had been a strange stroll. He had climbed

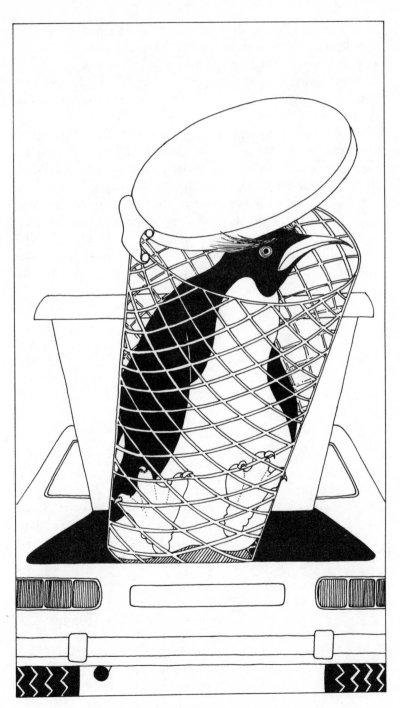

*A reveller picked up a penguin ...*

the fairground's big dipper, fallen off and had landed in Southport Zoo alongside the penguin compound. On an impulse, he scooped up the penguin, put it in a wire litter bin and dumped it in a friend's car boot. He did not tell the friend until he got home. 'At first he thought it was funny, but then he wasn't happy about it.'

So the next day the young man and his father took the penguin – which he had christened Percy – back to Southport and left it at a seafront car park in a plastic bucket, tipped on its side so that the bird could walk out. On hearing that the penguin had not been found, despite widespread land and sea searches, the culprit had been so distressed he had given himself up. 'I became very fond of the little fellow,' he said. The Bench fined him £100 and ordered him to pay £600 compensation, the value of the missing penguin.

# THE WORLD'S SECOND RICHEST DOG

Canine movie star Rin Tin Tin earned some $44,000 a picture and died in the arms of Jean Harlow in 1932, aged fourteen, after appearing in fifty films. Found abandoned as a puppy in a front-line trench in France during World War I, he was known as 'the mortgage lifter' for his money-making services to the studio where he was employed, Warner Brothers.

Over thirty years later, the mutt's estate filed suit against film-maker Michael Winner, claiming that the latter's movie, *Won Ton Ton, the Dog Who Saved Hollywood*, was based on Rin Tin Tin's own life story. Winner commented at the time: 'It's absurd to be sued by a dog, especially by a dog who has been dead for the past twenty years.'

# CAT WITH TEN LIVES

What is 'unnecessary suffering' within the meaning of the 1911 Protection of Animals Act? That question arose for decision in a case at Derby Magistrates' Court in 1986.

A local unemployed man had tried to drown a ten-day-old kitten because it had been rejected by its mother and was thought to be too sickly. He held it under water for fifteen minutes, and then buried it in a piece of waste ground. Unfortunately for him, but fortunately for the kitten, a neighbour had witnessed the whole scene. She called the police and the poor bedraggled creature was disinterred after some forty minutes, still breathing.

Had the man caused the kitten 'unnecessary suffering', as he later stood charged in court? No, ruled the Bench. The Chairman explained: 'We are of the opinion that the defendant believed the kitten to be dead when he buried it.' A lucky escape for the man, you might think – and an even luckier one for the kitten.

# HAZARD OF THE JOB

'Does your dog bite?' Inspector Clouseau asked as he reached down to pet the cuddly canine. 'No,' the innkeeper replied.

'Ouch,' the bumbling detective yelled, after being bitten. 'I thought you said your dog doesn't bite.'

'He's not my dog.'

If that scene had taken place in real life rather than in a Peter Sellers' movie, Inspector Clouseau would have needed to find the dog owner if he wanted to sue someone to pay for his injuries. And he would also have needed to prove that the dog had already bitten someone else – so that its owner would have had warning of his pet's dangerous propensity. The 'one bite' theory of canine liability.

However, ever since 1931, State legislation in California has amended the traditional Common Law ruling so that dog owners are generally liable for personal injury, even if it is their pet's first bite. The only exception is when the injured party has 'assumed the risk' of being bitten.

In March 1985, the 3rd District State Court of Appeal had to rule whether this applied to veterinary surgeons and their assistants when accepting dogs for treatment. One Rebecca Nelson, who worked as a veterinary assistant at an animal hospital in the divinely-named Paradise, a small mountain community in Butte County, California, was helping her boss with some minor surgery on Amos, a black 100lb labrador – in the summer of 1982. Amos had just been sedated. The dog appeared calm. Then, without any warning, it lunged at Rebecca and bit her in the face. She needed plastic surgery to remove the scars.

But could she sue the dog's owner? 'No', ruled the court. The normal rule of strict liability did not apply. She had 'assumed the risk of injury' by accepting her job as a veterinary assistant. 'Dog bites are an occupational hazard in the veterinary profession,' said the presiding judge.

# GOING TO LAW

Some people will go to court over almost anything. So it is only to be expected that animal disputes have led to some interesting courtroom cases.

In Bonn, West Germany, in November 1985, there was a surprisingly swift ending to a dispute that had raged for some three years. Over that time, two widows had been fighting over the ownership of a parrot named Coco. Frau Gretha Maier said she recognised her lost pet in the window of the home of one Frau Kristine Schmidt. But she could not prove ownership.

Then Coco himself was brought into court. He suddenly spoke out – and gave such a perfect imitation of Frau Maier that the judge promptly awarded the bird to her.

There was not such a happy ending in a Chicago courtroom in 1979, when a police officer was found guilty of contempt for refusing to get rid of his thirty-five pet ducks which his estranged wife said were keeping the couple apart. For four years the duck pond on the couple's property had been his delight, but the incessant quacking apparently was too much for his wife. She told the judge that her husband still came to feed the ducks every day and said he would never get rid of them.

The judged ruled otherwise and the police officer was given a week to part with his feathered friends under pain of imprisonment.

Another couple falling out over an animal led to that animal's death in Haverhill, Suffolk. A twenty-one-year-old man gave his common law wife a dog for Christmas back in 1979, and then almost at once regretted his decision. As he later explained to the police: 'The animal replaced me in her eyes. It even slept between us in bed. I just hated that dog.' So he killed it, and was not only fined £150 for cruelty but was also banned from owning another dog for ten years.

It was a tabby tom cat from next door that led to a retired major landing in court in Williton, Somerset, in September 1985.

The old soldier had seen service in India, Israel and Egypt, but had seen nothing to play on his nerves so much as this marauding moggy in Minehead where he lived. He had been trying to get shot of him for three years, ever since 'Tom' scented a victory of his own over the major's cat, a female.

In his eagerness to make a conquest, Tom would bolt through the neighbour's windows, if the door was shut, and go on the rampage upstairs and down. On these frequent visits he showed that, whatever he was like at home, he was not house-trained when at the major's. Cushions and carpets were ruined and furniture damaged. The major and his wife were in despair 'about keeping their home together', their solicitor later said. They 'threw shoes at it and they threw stones at it,' he told the Bench. 'In fact, anything that you normally throw at a cat was thrown but it kept coming back.'

Tom's lives, however, were all used up. The next time the cat sneaked onto his property, the major changed his

tactics and reached for his shotgun. Over the garden fence, the tabby's owner, a seventy-year-old woman, heard a bang. 'Have you shot the cat?' she demanded. 'Yes, I have,' replied her neighbour, who had, it was said, complained to her in the past about her pet, but without satisfaction.

In court, the major admitted unlawfully killing the cat; but was conditionally discharged. The Chairman of the Bench, who did not disclose whether she herself owned a cat, told him: 'You were under a certain amount of provocation'.

In April 1978, a small, white-haired woman lost a four-year fight and around £500 of her life-savings when two High Court judges blocked her continuing search for the missing bodies of her two feline friends: Pixie and Minkie Lou. They had been her two treasured pets. Minkie Lou had died in 1956 at the age of sixteen and Pixie had followed her to that great cattery in the sky four years later, at the age of twenty.

Both cats were buried in oak and mahogany caskets in a neighbour's garden because their owner, living alone in a flat at Streatham High Road, London, had no garden of her own. When the neighbours moved from Streatham to Mitcham a few miles away, they could not find the caskets and told the woman a 'white lie' that the cats had been re-buried at their new home.

She did not believe their story – as was, indeed, the case – and started a long legal battle against them claiming return of the caskets. It was never made quite clear exactly what she thought they had done with them. Anyway, she managed to lose two separate actions in the High Court, and failed to get the decisions reversed when she took her case to the Court of Appeal.

The casket-chaser was undeterred. 'I am an animal lover,' she said. 'I shall devote the rest of my life to finding the caskets. I now have a garden where I can bury them, if I find them.' I only hope she did.

# PARKING THE RHINO

When a motorist in Ipswich, Suffolk, was given a parking ticket by a traffic warden, one fine day in 1972, he said: 'I had a rhinoceros with me – did you expect me to carry it?'

Later, in the local magistrates' court, he explained that he was a sculptor and the rhinoceros was a 30lb steel model, which he produced as an exhibit to the Bench. He told the magistrates that he was delivering the rhino to a shop, and denied a parking offence. The Bench took his point and dismissed the summons.

# WHERE THERE'S A WILL

Who but an Englishman with the splendid name of Mr Pamplin Maudlin Vitner would leave £15,000 to be kept in trust for his two cats? Who but an English spinster would leave one half of the net proceeds of the sale of her house to another spinster 'for her to use at her discretion for her work for the welfare of cats and kittens needing care and attention' in a will taken to the English courts – and upheld – in the late 1940s? Who but an eccentric, wealthy American woman, such as Eleanor B. Ritchey, heiress to the Quaker State Refining Corporation, who died in Fort Lauderdale, Florida in 1968, would leave her entire estate, then worth $4.5 million, to her 150 stray dogs? By the time her will had been contested – inevitably – by relatives and been settled in September 1973, the estate had grown in value to $14 million and only seventy-three of the 150 dogs were still living.

It was another such lonely American woman, a childless widow of Charlotte, North Carolina, who left her $250,000 estate to her two canaries, Gigi and Co-Co, and her tom cat, Tommie. Gigi was later found dead and foul play by her co-inheritor, Tommie the cat, was suspected. The estate's attorney ordered a post-mortem and put a close watch on the surviving Co-Co. But all turned out well: the post-mortem revealed that Gigi had died a natural death. Tommie had not murdered his fellow beneficiary; he hardly needed to, his supply of fresh cream was guaranteed even if he led ninety-nine lives.

Joseph, a Burmese cat belonging to an elderly British widow, was also remembered in its mistress's will – although not quite so generously. His 'legacy' was only

*... his bed would be warmed by a miniature hot-water bottle*

£500, left to a friend of the dead woman on condition that the money would be spent on taking care of Joseph. What would be his diet? He would live on a regimen of fish, rabbit, crunchy cereal, chicken and a hot milk drink at night, and his bed would be warmed by a miniature hot water bottle. 'I suppose people might think it is silly to do all this for a cat, but that is what he is used to and I promised the old lady I would not let her down,' said the friend.

I have no doubt that she looked after Joseph splendidly to the end of his life, even if by then the £500 had long been spent. But, in fact, few wills have any monitoring system built into them. The friend or relative inherits the money not for himself but to use it for the welfare of the animal – neither in Britain nor the United States can you leave the money direct to the animal itself. But then who is to make sure that it is indeed spent on cream for 'Bunnie' or super bones for 'Fido'? Nobody. In law, everyone is on their honour, with nothing to be done if they transgress.

One old lady in Washington DC left her entire estate for the support of her pet parakeet by her ageing black housekeeper, who was allowed to remain living in her old home as long as the parakeet survived. Thereafter, the money was to go to an educational charity. One day the housekeeper turned up at the Wills Registry Office carrying a box containing the dead parakeet. The clerk was so impressed by her honesty that he later confessed that he wished he had had the courage to suggest she hide the dead bird and buy another to pass off as the original, so she could go on living in the house.

A man in Memphis, Tennessee, was a very special case. He left his money to a human, not to look after an animal but for having got rid of one. Or two, to be precise. For he wrote in his will: 'I leave $5,000 to the nurse who removed a pink monkey from the foot of my bed and a further $5,000 to the cook at the hospital who removed snakes from my broth.' All part of the service no doubt.

# LOVE KNOWS NO BARRIERS

The police were involved in a riotous horsey scene in the rolling countryside of Berkshire, in October 1985. A sexy young stallion went on a wild rampage to get at a group of mares in an adjoining field. He smashed down fences, hurt his owner, badly injured other horses – and started a kidnap scare.

The five-hour reign of terror had begun when the super-stud colt charged through fencing to reach mares and geldings owned by a neighbour. In the mêlée, the colt's owner was kicked and had to be taken to hospital in an ambulance.

Before the rampaging colt was finally captured, the mares' owner called for help from a girl rider who kept her pony in a field nearby. But this only added to the chaos. While the girl was helping to cope with the hot-blooded stallion, her parents found her bicycle seemingly abandoned in a shed, and called the local police because they thought she had been abducted.

The pursuit of love also reared its ugly head in August 1985 in the Midlands, when officials from the Ministry of Agriculture were called in by worried RSPCA officials.

Nearly 200 Canada Geese and Khaki Campbell ducks had been found dead on five Midland lakes. The local experts were baffled, but the cause of the problem was soon discovered. The birds had been having too much loving and had all caught an animal form of herpes. In their weakened state the disease, which has not yet claimed a human fatality, served to kill them off.

# DONKEY RIDES

The Delhi police have found a new way of pressing animals into police service, which they tried out on New Year's Day, 1986. More than fifty men, hands tied and faces blackened, who had made asses of themselves the night before in drunken end-of-year brawls, were paraded through the streets of India's capital on donkeys. Some carried signs announcing: 'This is going to be the fate of bad characters in 1986.'

Police said they planned more processions of well-known 'bad characters' as a warning to local criminals. It was the first parade of its kind in the capital, although villagers in rural areas had sometimes used similar tactics on suspected wrong-doers. It's nice to know that sophisticated city folk can still learn a thing or two from their country cousins.

# POOPER SCOOPERS

'Pooper scoopers' are virtually a legal necessity for dog owners in New York and other American cities, where fines of up to $100 can be imposed on people who let their animals foul the streets and other public spaces. These pick-up devices range from disposable cardboard shovels to the long-handled 'Sooper Dooper Pooper Scooper', which allows you to clean up without bending over.

In the British Parliament in February 1985, the government announced that it was going to introduce a similar pilot scheme in the United Kingdom. Among the areas to adopt the scheme was the London Borough of *Barking*.

The outcome of the experiment will, no doubt, be awaited with particular interest by at least one dog lover, a twenty-seven-year-old inhabitant of Middlesbrough. In the same month as the government's announcement, this kind-hearted man took an abandoned alsatian with a broken leg to the People's Dispensary for Sick Animals after it was found tied to a lamp-post. As he stood in the treatment queue, a Council dog warden booked him for allowing the dog to foul the pavement.

He was subsequently fined £5 for the offence by local magistrates, but refused to pay because he said the dog was not his. He was sent to jail for five days for non-payment, and was only released after his wife paid the fine.

In Paris, the French have characteristically treated the problem with uncompromising logic. In 1977 the capital's mayor, Jacques Chirac, decreed that thenceforth Parisian canines should have their own special lavatory space in each street. They would have at their disposal an area of six square feet in the gutter of every block. The spot would be indicated by a big white cross on the pavement, and by an arrow and a dog figure painted at the appropriate place. Even cars would not be allowed to park on that sacred site. Sadly the trouble has been that the dogs have not understood the significance of the signs.

But the Chinese and the Icelanders have carried the problem to its ultimate solution. In both Peking and Reykjavik respectively, dogs in the street are simply not allowed, even on a lead: they are liable to be seized and killed by the authorities – whatever they may be doing at the time. The Icelanders have had this harsh law for the past sixty years as part of an effort to control the tapeworm that has plagued the country for centuries. The Chinese only introduced it in 1983 – more, one suspects, for the dogs' benefit than for the people's.

# CRUELTY TO PRAWNS

We know that in English law a mouse can feel fear (see 'The Mouse and the Snake'), and that it is an open question whether a goldfish can (see 'Beastly Laws'). But what about a live prawn in *Scottish* law? The question arose for decision in January 1974 at Duns Sheriff Court in Berwickshire.

The local Procurator Fiscal prosecuted a sixteen-year-old girl fish worker for ill-treating prawns contrary to the 1912 Protection of Animals (Scotland) Act. He described feelingly to the Sheriff how he watched the prawns jump about in seeming agony on the girl's hotplate and finally die.

Her solicitor then took the same point as was later to be argued in the English goldfish case that a prawn was outside the protection of the law because it was neither a 'domestic or captive animal', as required by Section 13 of this Scottish Act. Nor were prawns specified in another section referring to birds, fish and reptiles in captivity. 'Prawns are an insect!' he said triumphantly, after consulting a natural history textbook.

Sheriff Paterson adjourned the case for 'technical evidence to be brought'. Some weeks later, a spokesman for the Procurator Fiscal's department in Berwickshire explained the case was being abandoned 'due to difficulties in proving that unnecessary suffering was being inflicted on prawns, and especially the fact that experts disagreed on the question of whether prawns can suffer pain.'

So we still do not know the answer.

# FOOD FOR THOUGHT

I have eaten bulls' testicles in Spain as a delicacy after a country bullfight but I was not even tempted to eat dog or snake when in Hong Kong, although all three items were legal according to the laws of Spain and Hong Kong respectively.

In mainland China, the Chinese really love their dogs – stewed, fried or minced, and served with lots of chilli (though it is no longer legal to eat them). Braised dog in brown sauce is quite a favourite too, along with dog dumplings. You can even eat monkey's brains quite legally, if you want to, in Taiwan, that last outpost of General Chiang Kai-Shek's old China: you gather round a table with a live monkey tied up in a hole in the middle, then someone slices off the top of its head and you all tuck in.

In the United States, you can legally eat rattlesnake; rattlesnake cutlets are a 'gourmet dish'. In Britain horse-flesh is legally considered 'unfit for human consumption', but most definitely not so in France and Belgium. In Thailand, locusts are a perfectly acceptable dish: when, in 1985, a Thai building worker ate four bags of locusts as a snack in Bangkok and died, the cause of death was not that strange food itself but the insecticide in the locusts.

In France and India (where most of them come from anyway) frogs are a legal culinary delight. There is nothing to prevent you buying or eating them in the United Kingdom, but when Safeway Foodstores put frogs' legs on sale in 1984, they soon had to withdraw them because of protests from animal lovers worried about the inhumane treatment of frogs during processing. In October 1985, India formally banned cutting off the legs of live frogs for export following worldwide complaints: thenceforth, export licences would only be granted to those who killed the frogs by painless electrical shocks.

Queen Elizabeth II has legally eaten a roasted rodent, though whether she liked the taste has not been reported. It happened at a state dinner during her visit to Belize in October 1985. Gibnut or *cuniculus*, the meat of the paca, a two-foot-long jungle animal, is a much sought-after delicacy in that region, and it was duly served to Her Majesty. Onlookers noticed her merely picking at the food, but a fellow guest at the dinner was quoted as saying: 'Paca is quite delicious. It looks like a large rat or guinea pig but has a flavour between turkey and pork.' I'm content to take his word for it.

When a chef at a Japanese restaurant in London plunged a live female tortoise, six inches long, into boiling water after trying unsuccessfully several times to make it stick its head out so that it could be decapitated, it happened so quickly that an RSPCA officer who was there could not prevent it.

But the law's wrath was not thwarted. Five months later the chef was fined £50 at the Mansion House Magistrates' Court for causing 'unnecessary suffering' to the tortoise. Counsel for the RSPCA explained that, although it was 'not to everyone's taste', it was not the fact that the tortoise was to be eaten that concerned the Society, but the method employed to kill it.

Religion is not what it was throughout the world. Devout Orthodox Jews are strictly enjoined never to let pork or any part of a dead pig touch their lips. But in August 1985, the Israeli Agriculture Minister had to admit that in the previous year pork had accounted for just under ten per cent of all the meat eaten in his country.

In the same month an Israeli pork supplier admitted in the Haifa Magistrates' Court that he had indeed doubled

*... it was duly served to Her Majesty*

the price of pork sold to local butchers earlier that year, despite the government's strictly enforced anti-inflationary emergency price regulations. Yet he insisted that he had not broken the law because the regulations – understandably, in view of the religious implications – had not fixed a maximum price for pork. Accordingly, he explained, all he had done was price his product in line with the maximum allowed by the regulations for beef.

The judge accepted the argument, and acquitted him.

# THE MOUSE AND THE SNAKE

The question of whether a goldfish could or could not feel pain, left undecided in the Cardiff case (see 'Beastly Laws'), was resolved, so far as mice are concerned, in a case which came before the Bradford Magistrates' Court in 1981.

A python in a glass tank at a pet shop in that city had rejected all food for two or three weeks. The pet shop owner tried to whet its appetite with a dead mouse, but the snake was not interested. So her twenty-year-old daughter tried to tempt it with a live, tame mouse. The mouse cowered in the tank for just under five minutes, but the snake still did not respond. In fact, it eventually died of self-induced starvation.

But the RSPCA brought a summons against the pet shop owner's daughter for 'cruelly terrifying' the mouse and against her mother for permitting it, contrary to the 1911 Protection of Animals Act. But could the mouse have been 'terrified'?

Two veterinary surgeons, one for the prosecution and one for the defence, disagreed in their evidence. The first said that the mouse *had* been maintained unnecessarily in a state of terror, and should have been removed once the python made no move to eat it after two minutes. The other, however, said that if it had been 'terrified' it would have made violent, frantic attempts to escape. He did not think that it had really been frightened because 'it would have no conception of what a snake is.'

The decision: the mouse *could* experience fear, but had not done so in this case. Both summonses were dismissed, and the two women were awarded £300 costs against the RSPCA.

# CAT AMONG THE PIGEONS

The battle between cats and birds has been fought since the beginning of recorded time, without the issue often coming before a court. But in Knightsbridge Crown Court, in London in 1979, there was a case which proved to be of fascinating interest to a particular kind of bird lover: pigeon fanciers.

What had happened was that a pigeon fancier living in Streatham had been convicted by the Camberwell magistrates of causing 'unnecessary suffering' to Sparky, a neighbour's cat, who had lost an eye after being shot by the man with an air rifle. He had been fined £50 with £65 compensation.

But the pigeon fancier was defiant. He took his case to the Crown Court on appeal: 'I aimed between the eyes and am a pretty good shot,' he said. 'I definitely tried to kill it.' The reason: the marauding Sparky had raided his lofts several times and had once killed a racing pigeon worth £100.

His counsel waxed eloquent: 'Cats with birds are like lions with humans. When they get a taste of blood, they come back again and again and again. We are not asking for *carte blanche* to kill cats but, if this conviction stands, it will have very far reaching consequences: fanciers will be unable to protect their pigeons from cats. One may have sympathy for the cat but one cannot ignore the pigeon.'

And the Bench at Knightsbridge Crown Court could not ignore such a passionate plea. The conviction was quashed. Representatives of the Royal Pigeon Racing Association – under the patronage of Her Majesty the Queen – who sat in court throughout the hearing, later said they were relieved at the decision.

Alas for pigeon enthusiasts, the Knightsbridge case did not serve to help another fancier at Portishead, in the West Country, in January 1981, when he shot and killed a tom cat called Spike because it had killed his pigeons.

When he appeared in court at Long Ashton, near Bristol, he told the magistrates how he had been surrounded by women screaming at him as Spike lay dead in the road. 'It looked as if I was being attacked by the Mafia,' he said. Yet he was still fined a total of £75, ordered to pay £43 costs and bound over to keep the peace for a year. His gun was also confiscated.

# APEING MARRIAGE

At Croydon Crown Court, London, in July 1985, Judge Jean Graham Hall had to consider the question of male dominance in the monkey's matrimonial world.

In February, magistrates at Bromley had convicted the venerable Royal College of Surgeons' Research Establishment in Kent of causing unnecessary suffering to a ten-year-old monkey named Mone that shared a cage with her male mate, and was found unconscious one day through severe dehydration. The temperature in the room containing the cage had been unbearably hot: sometimes reaching 92°F. Hence, the Bromley magistrates' conviction.

On Appeal, Judge Graham Hall agreed that this was very hot indeed. However that was not the main reason for upholding the conviction. Sitting with two magistrates, she said: 'We find that the main reason for Mone's unnecessary suffering was male domination over an extended mating period, so that she was unable to drink.' The experts at the Research Establishment should have realised this fact of monkey matrimonial life, and should have taken greater pains to help Mone stand up to her mate.

Six months later, on yet further appeal to the High Court in London, the conviction was finally quashed; but we are still left in the dark about the facts of life among 'married' monkeys. Lord Justice Lloyd said that the Royal College of Surgeons had had no opportunity at the time of the Croydon Crown Court hearing of defending the allegation about male monkey dominance, and so the conviction could not stand. Monkey husbands can still hold their head high in an English court of law.

# MORE ANIMALS IN THE DOCK

Putting animals on trial did not only happen in medieval times. The practice has gone on well into the present century.

In 1922, there was a parade in the Elephant Battery Lines at Hyderabad, India. An elephant attached to the field gun batteries of Nizam, the local ruler, was marched into the square and fastened to two other elephants. The following sentence of a court martial which the animal had just attended was read from the charge sheet:

'Military Elephant Suleiman, No 37: YOU have in a fit of wicked temper, slain your kind mahout, Mohammed Ali, thus causing grief to his family, loss to the State, disgrace to the battery, and vexation to our most August Ruler, whose name be blessed. For this thy sin thou art sentenced to receive ten strokes of the chain and to forfeit thine arrack for seven days.'

Two elephants from the Nizam's police force, each under the command of its own mahout, then duly flogged Suleiman with ten strokes of a long iron chain. His screams shook the square. A Western reporter witnessing the scene was told that an elephant who has thus been paraded and flogged rarely repeats his offence. One can well believe it.

Horatala, a huge elephant with enormous tusks, which always led the famous Perahera procession at Kandy, in Ceylon, was executed in June 1938 after being formally found guilty in court of the murder of eight men. Appeals by the Governor and Buddhist associations to save its life were unsuccessful.

The animal was chained to a rubber tree and shot dead

*As soon as he lit up, a policeman stepped forward ...*

by a well-known local, Scottish-born sportsman. In the few moments before its death, it kept turning to face the rifle as though it knew its end was near.

But Westerners need not think they are so superior. 'We find the defendant guilty as charged' was the verdict returned by a jury at Pikeville in Kentucky in January 1926, in the case of 'the State $v$ Bill.' The defendant, a collie dog, had been formally indicted for being an animal of vicious character. Bill was brought into court and placed in the dock. Witnesses testified to its vicious character and, upon the jury's verdict, the judge solemnly pronounced sentence of death. Bill was later executed by the Public Executioner and his head sent to the Lexington Laboratory for examination.

A sheep in the village of Montzen, near Verviers, in Belgium in November 1930 was luckier.

The animal, driven to frenzy by children teasing it, pushed one of them, a four-year-old boy, into the river. The child died, and the animal's owner appeared before the Verviers judge – together with the sheep. Fortunately, both were discharged on the ground that the sheep lost its temper because the child had teased it.

Back in the United States in March 1923, a chimpanzee gave a performance at South Bend, Indiana and, among other tricks, he smoked a cigarette. As soon as he lit up, a policeman stepped forward and demanded the animal's name in order that a summons might be issued against him for infringing a law of the Indiana Legislature against cigarette smoking in public.

In court the following day it was pleaded that the chimpanzee could hardly be expected to know the extent of his guilt. But the magistrate ruled that ignorance was no excuse for breaking the law, and fined the defendant $5, which was promptly paid by its trainer.

In October 1913 a Pomeranian dog was sentenced to death in Newark, New Jersey, for the murder of a parrot. It was clearly shown on the evidence that the dog, irritated by the remarks of the parrot, which lived next door, had leaped the fence and killed the bird by biting it in the neck. The parrot's owner, a boy of thirteen, laid information against the dog and appeared personally in court to press for the death penalty. The judge duly obliged.

As recently as October 1977, a monkey was sentenced to death in Bogota, Colombia, for the murder of a woman.

Marco Polo, the country's most famous monkey and star of a popular children's television show, was ordered to be executed by Judge Clara Ines Acevado after he had savaged a seventy-year-old woman, who bled to death from her wounds. Three days later, however, the judge relented after the National Society for Animal Welfare said it would take charge of him. Lucky Marco Polo received an eleventh-hour reprieve.

Until then he had been held in police cells with twenty prostitutes and fifteen common criminals. The monkey, who was twenty inches tall, was kept on the end of a chain to prevent him attacking fellow inmates. A spokesman for the animal society which had hired a lawyer to defend him commented: 'There's no death penalty in Colombia for humans, let alone animals.'

# A LOT OF BULL

The bull is, I suppose, the animal most closely identified in the popular mind with rampant and aggressive sexual desires.

It is, therefore, appropriate that the title of 'Ireland's Greatest Lover' was given in the late 1970s to Hamlet, a seven-year-old bull at the Dublin District Milk Board Artificial Insemination Station, who had sired an estimated 75,000 offspring before dropping dead in his prime. The stringent legal framework within which the artificial insemination of bulls takes place (see 'Beastly Laws') had not served to avoid this sad event. The veterinary surgeon said that poor Hamlet had probably died of heart failure – 'as bulls in his line of work generally do.'

So much for the protection of the law!

It was the animal passions of a prize Holstein bull named Arab that, in July 1980, led to a fascinating five-day case in the High Court at Chester.

Some three years earlier, Arab, who lived on a farm at Doddleston in Cheshire, could not believe his good fortune when a herd of attractive cows strayed into his field from the adjoining farm. He reacted as any normal red-blooded bull would do and attempted to make the most of the situation. Unfortunately, he was still recovering from an injury that he had received a few months earlier while mating with twenty-six heifers at another nearby farm – and was really not up to the job.

As his owner feelingly said in court: 'He deteriorated rapidly after the night with the cows. The transformation was fantastic. I have never seen an animal transformed from such a magnificent specimen to a total wreck.'

Arab, who was still only four years old and who at one

time had been expected to earn as much as £1½ million in stud and artificial insemination fees during a twelve-year-long 'working' life, had to be destroyed. The once-proud lover ended up as sausages and soup, and his owner sued the adjoining farmer for his loss. He was reasonable in his claim, so he said, putting Arab's value at a 'realistic' assessment of £150,000.

Mr Justice Phillips ruled that, although the neighbouring farmer – a ninety-six-year-old retired headmistress – *was* liable for her cows' 'cattle trespass', a charming old English legal term, Arab's owner was not entitled to anything like £150,000. The trouble was that Arab, when tempted by the wandering cows, was already nothing like the bull he once had been. After hearing evidence from experts, his Lordship ruled that the earlier mishap with the twenty-six heifers had meant that his love-making days were over anyway. Even if the old lady's cows had not strayed, Arab would have had to have been destroyed.

In purely legal terms, the only financial loss that the bull's owner had suffered as a consequence of the 'cattle trespass' was some additional damage done to Arab in the course of his abortive rampage; that reduced the value of his carcass by only £147.76. That was all to which his suing owner was entitled.

The judge rounded up the proceedings by quoting from the poem 'Bull' by Ralph Hodgson, the nineteenth-century Yorkshire-born poet. His Lordship said that it was a fitting description of Arab's plight:

Pity him this fallen chief,
All his splendour, all his strength,
All his body's breadth and length,
Dwindled down with shame and grief,
Half the bull he was before,
Bones and leather, nothing more.

# MAN'S BEST FRIEND

Some things have not changed since the beginning of time. A skeleton, unearthed by workmen on a building site on the Sussex Downs at Woodingdean near Brighton in 1982, was identified as a Saxon who died more than 1,000 years earlier. His dog was buried at his feet.

When eighty-seven-year-old widow, Mrs Barbara Montague, died at Basingstoke, Hampshire, in 1981, her last wish was to be buried in her garden next to her pet corgi's grave. This caused a problem for the Basingstoke Council Planners. The Director of Planning said: 'This is a very rare application. I have never met it in all my years. I think it will be looked at favourably.'

And so it was. Some six weeks later it was announced that dear old Mrs Montague could rest forever beside her favourite dog.

Another dedicated dog lover was the woman of Pilgate, Lincolnshire, who when she read in the newspaper that an eight-year-old collie called Spot was to be destroyed by order of a court for biting people, felt she had to do all she could to prevent this.

For four months, at her own expense, she looked after the animal during an abortive appeal to Lincoln Crown Court. Only when this was lost, with legal costs of £1,300, was Spot taken to a vet. 'I looked after the dog for four marvellous months,' she said, 'and that is the time I will remember because he had the best of everything with long walks and good food, especially during those final days.'

*The body was placed in a specially made coffin ...*

Seventy-seven-year-old Commander Edmond Chapman –
who survived the sinking of the aircraft carrier *Courageous*
in 1939 – and his wife even went as far as leaving Britain
to save the lives of their two alsatian dogs.

Jake and Elsa were sentenced to death by magistrates
after they had attacked a couple of people. One of the
dogs then added to their problems by grabbing the jacket
of a policeman sent to investigate. 'England is my land,'
said the doughty Commander. 'I am not too fond of the
weather but I would have liked to stay here. But killing
the dogs is out of all proportion to the seriousness of what
happened.'

So he and his wife emigrated to France – and as they
boarded the cross-Channel ferry taking them into exile,
one of the alsatians tried to bite a Customs man!

But it's not only in Britain that people go potty about
poodles. In 1977, a dog was given the full funeral rites of
a human being when it died at a Buddhist monastery in
Upper Burma. The local abbot decided to give the dog a
proper Buddhist funeral because it seemed too intelligent
to be treated like an ordinary dog. The body was placed
in a specially made coffin and twelve Buddhist monks –
representing each year of the dog's life – then recited
religious verses. About 500 people attended the funeral.

# MISTAKEN IDENTITY

It is not only human defendants who sometimes claim, 'You've got the wrong one. It wasn't me.' The defence of mistaken identity was raised at Oxford Crown Court in February 1986, when the owner of Benjy, a boisterous mongrel who had sunk his teeth into a postman, denied the police charge that it was the animal's second offence – and that he should accordingly be destroyed as a 'dangerous dog' out of her control.

The dog's owner told the Court that the prosecution had got it all wrong. Their criminal records were all mixed up: 'Benjy's only done it once to the postman,' she said. 'The first time anyone got bitten was when my *other* dog, Susie, had a go at someone else.'

Prosecuting counsel chimed in to say that the police did now accept that it was Susie and not Benjy who had struck before. The result: the judge accepted that it was a genuine case of mistaken identity and quashed the destruction order. However, he added sternly to the ecstatic owner: 'You have now got two dogs who have not been kept under proper control. The fault lies with you, not the dogs – but it will be the dogs who will be destroyed if you don't control them!' In other words, the next bite could be their last.

# AMOROUS RAMS

The activities of two rams landed a Welsh farmer in court at Newport, in February 1983.

The animals had got among another farmer's flock of pure-bred Suffolk ewes and had allegedly serviced twenty-four of them in one evening. As a result, thirty-seven lambs were born some five months later, during the big freeze of January 1982, and seventeen died. The Welsh farmer claimed that it was 'simply not realistic' for two rams to service twenty-four ewes in eighteen hours. But the judge was not impressed. He ordered him to pay £600 damages and costs.

A human ram ended up going to prison for three months for adultery in Greece (where they still jail people for this!) in April 1982.

Pericles Alfonsos was in the habit of leaving home for one or two days, taking his rifle with him and telling his wife that he was going off hunting. He never failed to bring back game for the dinner table. One night, Mrs Alfonsos invited her father to join them for dinner to eat a duck that her husband claimed he had shot on one of these successful outings. Sadly for Pericles, his father-in-law knew the difference in taste between a fresh duck and a frozen one.

He told his daughter of his suspicions and, on Pericles' next trip, the two of them followed him – and saw him walk into the flat that he kept for his mistress!

# SNAKES ALIVE!

In July 1983, a London busker appeared at Marylebone Magistrates' Court charged with contravening a railway bye-law by 'performing a magic trick with an Indian python snake and interfering with the comfort of passengers' between Paddington and Edgware Road stations on the London Underground.

A police constable solemnly told the Bench that the busker, dressed in shorts, a bra and blouse, with fishnet stockings and his face painted as a clown, shouted greetings to passengers as he boarded the train. He started performing 'childish magic tricks' with a teddy bear and a theatrical pistol. 'The loud bang of the pistol shocked some of the female passengers,' said the constable.

The busker 'then asked if anyone had a whistle. There was no response, so he produced one himself. He played the whistle and a large snake began rising from the straw shopping basket. Several passengers quickly moved away stating their disturbance and fears over the snake, which was now coiled round [the busker's] shoulders and neck.'

The busker moved around the passengers talking about the 'Monty Python Magic Show' and 'obviously causing fear to some'. When the train eventually pulled into the next station, several people asked him to leave and many complained to rail staff. By this time the busker had collected £1.45 in a hat.

The defendant told the Court: 'Obviously I wouldn't have taken £1.50 in a train carriage if I wasn't being appreciated.' The magistrates must have agreed, for they did not fine him but merely gave him a year's conditional discharge.

Did the resourceful busker commit a criminal offence merely by having the six-foot-long python as a pet? Not at all. It's still a free country. The 1976 Dangerous Wild Animals Act allows you to have any non-poisonous snake – such as pythons and boa constrictors – as your very own personal friend. The only qualification is that it must be your own property. A twenty-eight-year-old builders' labourer in Berkshire landed in court at Newbury in June 1980 because he had overlooked this vital legal point. In fact, he had stolen a baby boa constrictor from a nearby pet shop and hidden it under the floorboards in his bathroom.

Somehow the local police force were alerted, and it cost him a £100 fine and £25 costs. He could have bought the snake for £52.

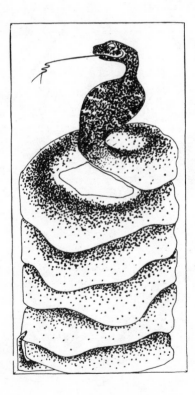

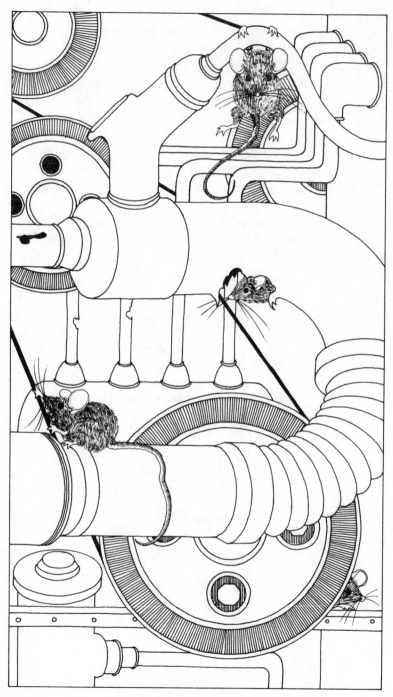

*Taking the mickey*

# TAKING THE MICKEY

In 1983 a motorist in Dyfed, Wales, was extremely angry when his car refused to start two days after he got it back from a service. He was even angrier when the garage charged him £30 to rectify the problem – and blamed mice.

He complained to the local Trading Standards Department, only to find that an investigation cleared the garage. Microscopic examination of the replaced fuel pipes and spark plug caps revealed mice teeth marks, and officials who visited his garage at home found tell-tale mice droppings on the floor.

# HEDGEHOG HATER

A twenty-nine-year-old man living in Herne Bay, Kent, considered that hedgehogs were 'vermin'. He simply could not stand them. So when he found a hedgehog rummaging in his rubbish bins, he attacked it with a broom handle. When the animal curled up to protect itself, he carried on hitting it 'as if playing golf'. To be fair to him, he later admitted that he was drunk at the time.

However, the RSPCA got to hear of the incident and prosecuted the man for cruelty to an animal, under the 1911 Protection of Animals Act. This raised the question of whether a hedgehog was 'a domestic or captive animal' within the meaning of that Act. The Canterbury magistrates ruled that it was neither. So, they threw out the case.

Subsequently, the chairman of the British Hedgehog Preservation Society, comprising some 6,000 members, said that the acquittal was a travesty of justice and that he would complain to the Lord Chancellor that the Act was clearly inadequate. No doubt the shade of the poor battered hedgehog would agree.

# BLACK AND WHITE

At Swansea Crown Court in November 1982, Judge Michael Gibbon, QC ruled that a champion-dog breeder had been tricked over the love-match of her prize white poodle bitch.

He awarded £900 damages to a seventy-four-year-old Miss Helen Martin, who had brought along her pure white six-year-old poodle bitch, Caro, full name Champion Martindell Carolina, to the kennels of an established poodle-breeder for mating with his pure white poodle stud, Lentella My Way, nicknamed Geoffrey. The animal had been described in a breeders' magazine as 'an outstanding white male of great presence' available to approved bitches.

But something went wrong. After drinks and lunch in the poodle-breeder's flat, Miss Martin, accompanied by friends, went down to a courtyard to see the mating. Perhaps because it was Caro's first experience of this nature, she snarled and snapped; for his part, My Way appeared equally uninterested. So Miss Martin accepted the poodle-breeder's suggestion that she should return to the flat and leave the two animals to get on with it in her absence. Some time later he joined her and said that there had been a 'very successful mating'.

And so there had. Six weeks later Caro gave birth to a litter of six puppies. The only trouble was that they were all jet black!

Miss Martin could not register them at the Kennel Club, and she claimed they were worth only £45 each, instead of the £250 which white puppies would have fetched. She sued for her money. With whom had Caro been mated while her mistress waited upstairs?

In court, the poodle-breeder maintained that it had

indeed been the highly respectable My Way. He said that perhaps there might have been some 'accident' in Miss Martin's own kennel. The plaintiff's counsel told the judge that the case was a tragedy rather than farce. He quoted from Shakespeare's *Othello* to illustrate the tragic theme: 'Now, even now, a black ram is tupping your white ewe.' He even considered it necessary to quote Jonathan Swift's description of lawyers as 'men trained from an early age to prove that black is white, or white black, according as they are paid.'

I am not sure how Judge Gibbon reacted to that remark; but it did not prevent him ruling that the unfortunate Caro had, in fact, not known the joys of love with My Way but with a standard poodle, probably substituted for the temperamental would-be groom by the breeder. The learned judge said that the man had told 'a white lie' to protect his dog's reputation. Unfortunately, he had not realised that the chances of two white poodles producing six black puppies were as remote as nearly ten million to one.

# TRADING STANDARDS

It is the task of the diligent officers of local authorities' Trading Standards Departments throughout Britain to enforce the 1968 Trade Descriptions Act. Primarily, of course, this deals with goods and services sold to the general public. But animals come within the definition of 'goods', and this leads to some interesting cases.

In 1975, a woman who bought a gelding called Goody Two Shoes at Gloucester Market noticed that it was displaying 'stallion tendencies'. She reported her discovery to the local Trading Standards Department, and the seller was fined £20 by Cheltenham magistrates for applying a 'false trade description' to the horse, which was, in fact, a stallion.

In Welshpool, a local businessman who tried to market his 'Hedgehog Crisps' was told by local officials that he must take them off his shelves because the crisps did not contain any hedgehog. But he soon started selling them again – once he had changed the pack to make it clear that the hedgehog flavouring was only artificial!

'There is no legal definition of "free range" eggs,' the Chief Trading Standards Officer for Shropshire told the Shrewsbury Magistrates in May 1982 when asking them to make a ruling that would stand as a precedent.

A local farmer was before the court, charged with supplying eggs with a 'false trade description', in that he had called them 'free range' when, in fact, he operated a 'deep litter' system. This meant that, although the hens were held in sheds holding up to 1,200 birds, they were not enclosed within battery cages. They ran free in the sheds and had access to pasture through 'popholes' in the sides.

The officer maintained that this was not 'free range' as the average consumer would have understood it. He maintained that 'free range' could only describe eggs laid by birds who had 'unrestricted access to pastureland, moving about at will and getting a substantial part of their food from natural sources.'

What was the answer? The magistrates agreed with the officer and convicted the farmer, who was fined £100. 'Free range' means free range – in the open.

One of the achievements of the Hertfordshire Trading Standards Department in 1981 was to investigate a complaint that a veterinary surgeon had overcharged by claiming £20 for his visit to a sick dog. It 'seemed excessive', said the department in its annual report, because the animal was already dead when he arrived. The bill was reduced.

# DIRTY DOG

A dog owner was shamed before his friends when a Torquay solicitor served a paternity suit on him at a dinner-dance in November 1981. The culprit was his black poodle, Ossie, who had made the solicitor's pedigree terrier pregnant.

The solicitor later explained: 'My wife had set her heart on Puff having pedigree offspring, so I was determined that if there were going to be a lot of mongrel pups Ossie was not going to get away with it. I made out an affiliation order and presented it to his owner at a social function we both attended. It was worth losing Puff's pedigree to see his face.'

All ended amiably. Ossie's owner said: 'I have admitted liability on my dog's behalf and have promised to pay maintenance of tins of dog food.'

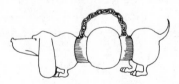

# ANIMAL JUDGEMENTS

British judges are renowned for their felicitous use of the English language. They are very fond of metaphor and descriptive turns of phrase. Lord Sumner, in the post-World War I days, was an outstanding example of this trend.

In *Board of Trade v Hain Steamship Co Ltd*, in 1929, he had to decide whether a collision between a warship and another ship some six weeks after the Armistice had been signed on 11 November 1918 was the result of warlike operations. Counsel had argued that it was not, because the warship had been engaged on the peaceful errand of taking mines back to her parent country, but Lord Sumner observed:

'I recognise the high importance of considering the ship's errand and the purpose of her voyage, but I should have thought that, having proved an animal at large to be a lion, it was not further indispensable to prove that he was not at the moment merely performing as a lamb, unless, of course, some circumstances of ovine behaviour happened to be apparent.'

In another case in 1934, when the Court of Appeal was considering a humdrum ruling on the meaning of 'good-will' when a business was sold, Lord Justice Scrutton opined that the subject must be considered on a 'cat, dog and rat' basis.

'The cat prefers the old home to the person who keeps it, and stays in the old home when the person who has kept the house leaves. The cat represents that part of the customers who continue to go to the old shop, though the old shopkeeper has gone; the probability of their custom may be regarded as an additional value given to the premises by the tenant's trading.

'The dog represents that part of the customers who follow the person rather than the place; these the tenant may take away with him if he does not go too far.

'There remains a class of customer who may neither follow the place nor the person, but drift away elsewhere. They are neither a benefit to the landlord nor the tenant, and have been called "the rat" for no particular reason except to keep the epigram in the animal kingdom. I believe my brother, Maugham, has introduced the rabbit, but I will leave him to explain the position of the rabbit.'

Lord Justice Maugham (whose true brother was Somerset Maugham, the writer) readily took up the challenge. '"The rabbit" indicates the customers who come simply from propinquity to the premises; and, if this is borne in mind it will be apparent that the rabbit may be much bigger than the cat, who (if indeed it does not wholly vanish) may well shrink to the dimensions of a mouse.'

What on earth all this 'Animal Farm' terminology had to do with a case on landlord and tenant is anybody's guess.

In 1954 Sheriff Hector McKechnie, QC had to consider the legal consequences of the antics of a particularly high-spirited cow at the auction market in Inverness. The animal had got out into the street through an unsecured gate, climbed a stairway over a shop, fallen through the upper floor into the premises below and, in her struggles, turned on a tap – which flooded the place.

The shopkeeper's claim against the auctioneers failed, however, for Sheriff McKechnie felt himself 'forced to the conclusion that a gate-crashing, stair-climbing, floor-bursting, tap-turning cow is something strictly of its own kind, for whose depredations the law affords no remedy unless there was foreknowledge of some such propensities.'

# MORE BEASTLY LAWS

Of all the countries in the world, the United States must surely have the strangest set of animal laws. Here are just a few examples:

In Pine Island, Minnesota, a man must remove his hat when meeting a cow.

In Arkansas, it is illegal to blindfold a cow on public roads.

In Vermont, you cannot engage in the business of raising, breeding, keeping or maintaining horses for the purpose of selling their urine, unless you have a licence to do so.

In Massachusetts, you must not travel on a way with a sleigh or sled drawn by a horse, unless the harness has at least three bells attached to it.

In Berea, Ohio, the owner of every animal out on the streets after dark must ensure that it wears a tail light.

In Michigan, you must not tie a crocodile to a hydrant.

In New Hampshire, if you steal, take or carry away someone else's bear without his permission, you are guilty of a misdemeanour.

In Washington DC, anyone owning or keeping five or more mammals, larger than a guinea pig and older than four months, must obtain an Animal Hobby Permit – but this does not apply to a licensed pet shop, licensed veterinary hospital, circus or travelling exhibition.

In Natchez, Mississippi, you are not allowed to let your elephant drink beer.

In Kentucky, anyone who uses any kind of reptile for the purpose of a religious service can be fined between $50 and $100.

# JAIL-DOG

A cat and dog fight does not usually lead to either animal serving a prison term, but it happened to Pep, a male labrador retriever in Pike County, Pennsylvania, back in 1924.

Pep, usually a quiet, friendly dog, suddenly went wild one hot summer's day and killed a cat that – just his bad luck! – happened to belong to the State Governor's wife. The enraged Governor presided over an immediate hearing and then trial. Without benefit of legal representation, the unfortunate Pep was sentenced to life imprisonment.

He was duly delivered to the state penitentiary where a bewildered warden had no idea what to do with him. Should he give him an identity number, as with all new entrants? He decided that he should, and the dog duly posed for a prison mug-shot.

Pep, Prisoner No C2559 served six years (forty-two dog years) in jail before dying of old age. It is nice to know that they were happy years: his fellow prisoners lavished him with gifts and he was allowed to change cells whenever he wanted to.

# ANIMAL FARM

All the world loves a lover – but the English prefer their animals. That is the essential truth that anyone studying the English law of animals must at once appreciate.

It is not without significance that as long ago as 1822 Parliament passed the first law making cruelty to animals a crime, whereas it took MPs another sixty-seven years to get around to making cruelty to children also an offence. The Royal Society for the Prevention of Cruelty to Animals – notice that *Royal* – dates from 1824. The *National* Society for the Prevention of Cruelty to Children dates from 1884.

British courts are notoriously lenient to child-beaters. To arouse their true anger an animal must be hurt. As in the classic case some years ago of the old man sitting in the sun in London's Hyde Park who was annoyed by a puppy dancing around his feet. 'Viciously' he stamped on it with his foot. The puppy yelped – and the Marlborough Street magistrate sent the old man to jail for six weeks. Some time later, a young Kent farmer broke his three-month-old baby son's arm and fractured eight of his ribs. 'This was a terrible and serious thing,' said the chairman of the local Bench. And fined him £20 with £5 costs.

English law divides animals into wild and domestic. The owner of a wild animal is responsible automatically for any damage that it causes: in the words of academic lawyer, Sir John Salmond, 'He who keeps a dangerous animal keeps it at his peril.' But with a domestic animal the injured party must first prove either negligence or that the owner knew the particular animal had a specific tendency to do dangerous things.

This division can sometimes be somewhat arbitrary. In the early years of World War II, when a child visiting a zoo was bitten while feeding a camel, the Court of Appeal ruled confidently: 'There is nowhere in the world a camel which is wild and not domesticated.' The girl's father could not prove the zoo knew of any similar incident with *its* camel. So she lost her case.

But in January 1954 some tame and well-mannered circus elephants were frightened by a dog yapping at their heels. They stampeded and trampled on a midget, badly shocking his wife. It was not the elephants' fault, nor the circus owners' nor their trainer's. But two years later, in the High Court, Mr Justice Devlin made Bertram Mills Circus Limited pay damages because an elephant was, in law, a wild animal – even though these particular elephants were tame and normally no more dangerous than a cow.

Never for one moment should anyone think that English law is consistent. Any hen, goose, sheep, cattle, horse, ass or pig is thought better of than a human being. According to the Animals Act of 1971, if a dog attacks any of these creatures its owner automatically has to pay damages, whether or not it was the first time. As Lord Goddard once said: 'In English law a sheep is better protected than a baby.'

Yet if a dog attacks another dog, the injured hound's owner has to prove an earlier attack. 'Dog does not bite dog', ruled Judge Brian Grant in a 1967 case, when a dachshund's owner unsuccessfully sued an alsatian's owner for damage to his pet.

But if a *cat* attacks a hen, goose, sheep, cattle, etc, there is no liability whatsoever – whether this is the first, second or third attack! Follow the legal logic of that, if you can.

# SELF DEFENCE

Self-defence is a fundamental principle of every system of law.

You are entitled to use 'reasonable force' to withstand attack. Indeed, Lord Morris of Borth-y-Gest, a senior English law lord, said most helpfully in a Privy Council case in November 1970: 'If in a moment of unexpected anguish a person has only done what he honestly and instinctively thought was necessary, that would be most patent evidence that only reasonably defensive action has been taken.'

This salutory principle has been applied not only to human beings in relation to animals, but also with animals in relation to human beings. When, in September 1982, the Stipendiary Magistrate at Clerkenwell Court, London, was told that a twenty-five-year-old local dog owner had given his mongrel a sniff of glue in a park 'for a laugh', the distinguished lawyer was so outraged that he commented: 'My only regret is that the dog didn't bite you.' He had to content himself with merely fining the joker £60 and ordering him to pay £25 costs.

In Blankenberge, Belgium, a man was charged with assault in June 1977 after repeatedly biting a dog which got into a fight with his own dog. He only stopped biting when the injured dog's owner, a woman, hit him over the head with her handbag.

In New Zealand, in 1985, there was a most successful case of self-defence by a duck. A hunter loosed off both barrels of his shotgun at the innocent creature flying above him – and missed. Whereupon the duck circled, returned and

*... a most successful case of self-defence*

dive-bombed the hunter. It flew straight into his face, breaking his nose, glasses and a tooth.

Even babies get into the act. In Melbourne, Australia, in February 1980, the parents of eighteen-month-old Diane Stiles ran into the garden of their suburban home when they saw Diane chewing happily on a venomous black snake. But the baby, who had been teething, was fine – she had already killed the snake by biting through its head.

# GROUNDS FOR DIVORCE

I don't know if anyone has actually got married because of a pet animal, but there certainly have been cases where marriages have broken up because of one.

One such case ended up in the Divorce Court in London in the early seventies because a young husband, living in Staines, Middlesex, moved a chair to make way for a visitor in front of the television set and inadvertently stepped on the family dog. The animal yelped and the husband didn't say 'Sorry' to it – whereupon his wife attacked and punched him in front of the guest, and screamed that she would do no more cooking for him. Things went downhill from there.

Judges seem to share a soft spot for pooches. The Court of Appeal once had to consider a dispute where a husband from another part of Middlesex, vexed with his wife because he believed she had carelessly allowed his white miniature poodle bitch to mate with her black poodle, threw the bitch at her and said: 'She's your responsibility now.'

Did those words constitute a gift of the poodle to the wife?

Her counsel told the three Appeal Court judges that it was a 'comparatively trifling matter'. But Lord Justice Edmund Davies – who had sternly sentenced some of the Great Train Robbers to thirty years apiece some while previously – did not agree: 'It is no use,' he said, 'telling at least two members of the Court that a dispute over a dog is a matter of little importance. Few could be graver.'

That certainly was the view taken by a former model from Rickmansworth, Herts, who, when her childless marriage to an electrician broke up in July 1979, refused to hand over the family's three-year-old collie, Gypsy, to her husband – despite a Court order giving him 'custody' of the animal.

She claimed that she had given the dog away. 'If that was so,' said her husband's counsel, it showed 'a lack of understanding about men and their pets' and revealed 'total insensitivity'.

It would seem that Judge Colin Sleeman didn't believe her because he ordered her to reveal the dog's whereabouts to her estranged husband within fourteen days, or else go to jail for a week for contempt of court.

# OFF WITH THEIR HEADS

France abolished the guillotine for humans in 1981, but some four years earlier it was in use in Italy as a form of execution – for pigeons.

In March 1977 the pigeons in Siena were proving themselves a positive menace. They were carrying a form of salmonella which could be dangerous to man. The town's left-wing city council took prompt action. They decided that every one of the city's 4,000 and more pigeons would be guillotined.

The Socialist mayor, Canzio Vannine, explained to reporters: 'Guillotining has been approved as the most humane way of destroying the birds after consultation with local animal protection society officials.' One wonders who their patron was: Robespierre?

# CAVEAT EMPTOR

*Caveat Emptor* is that fine old Latin tag that encapsulates a vital principle of Anglo-American Contract Law. It means 'Let the Buyer Beware'. As a general rule, subject to statutory exceptions and in the absence of fraud, it is for the buyer to make sure that he gets what he wants rather than for the seller to try and read his mind for him.

This exemplary principle was clearly shown in a prosecution, in September 1970, for an alleged breach of the 1968 Trade Description Act. The licensee of a public house at Bollington in North Cheshire was charged before the local magistrates with selling a guard dog, named Rebel, 'to which a false trade description was applied' in that it was alleged to have been a trained guard dog when it was not.

The Bench heard how an antiques shopowner had decided to get a guard dog when her shop was broken into for the third time. She saw an advertisement in an evening newspaper in which the licensee offered to supply 'companion alsatian guard dogs to suit licensed or business premises, also pet alsatians to suit a family.' So she visited his premises, and came away with Rebel.

Unfortunately, Rebel did not seem to be very good at his job. A police sergeant in charge of training dogs for the Cheshire Police was called in to test the animal's ability. It failed abysmally. As the sergeant gently opened the antiques dealer's kitchen door, Rebel stirred, 'sauntered' up to him and then backed away, returning to its corner to lie down.

A conviction would have seemed inevitable. But the magistrates threw out the case when they accepted that the licensee had actually tried to persuade the antiques dealer to buy a guard dog called Simba, but she insisted on choosing another one, although he had told her that it was not a guard dog.

By a strange coincidence, it was another 'too friendly' guard dog named Rebel that figured in a fascinating case in Hull some sixteen years later. The owner of a local secondhand shop bought an alsatian dog after his store had been raided five times in three weeks. But the hapless hound was simply not up to the job. When the thieves returned a sixth time, they stole the dog!

# BATS IN THE RAFTERS

The demise of a colony of bats roosting in the rafters of a century-old cottage in North Yorkshire resulted, in February 1986, in a piece of legal history.

The owner of a local timber treatment company became the first person in England to be prosecuted for intentionally killing a bat. A special sitting of the Bedale Magistrates' Court heard that the timber treatment expert had only intended to destroy woodworm lurking in the roof timbers of the cottage, but that the spray his workmen used also proved fatal to a colony of Brandt's bats. They dropped from their roosting places in the rafters into the watertank in the loft, and their fragmented remains eventually trickled out through the kitchen tap.

The Bench duly imposed a fine of £500 with £200 costs, and afterwards the bewildered expert said: 'I am extremely disappointed. Those bats have given me nightmares for months. From now on I will inspect every attic on my hands and knees so I don't miss any sign of bats.'

Why look down for them and not up at the ceiling? Because the sure give-away for bats in the rafters – or in the belfry – is the evidence of their droppings on the floor.

# BAA BAA BLACK SHEEP

In 1982, a prosperous businessman in Münster, West Germany, hit on a novel idea for 'mowing' the lawn of his luxuriously converted farmhouse outside the city. He bought a small flock of sheep to do the job.

No problem – at least, for three years. Then came a letter from the local farmers' co-operative, claiming that he had been a member of their organisation ever since he bought the sheep. The businessman replied that this was nonsense. He had nothing against farmers' co-operatives, as such, but he was most certainly not a member. 'But you are!' replied the co-operative, pointing out that ownership of the sheep had made him a sheep farmer – and that he owed them about 1,500DM in back dues.

That was not all. As a sheep owner, the bemused businessman learned, he was entitled to agricultural subsidies from both the West German government and the European Community; the amounts involved would more than cover his co-op fees and he could also get a free trip to a spa if injured while tending his animals; and if he died, his widow would receive a pension in the region of 1,000DM for the rest of her life.

Such news would perhaps have delighted most people, but not Herr Gunter Röttgering, for he combined his business career with active membership of the Christian Democratic Party's National Committee on Subsidy Abuses; and this seemed just such an abuse. He investigated further and discovered that the various farming co-operatives routinely recruited people like himself, apparently to bolster depleted ranks and bank balances. When last heard of, the worthy Herr Röttgering had just begun legal proceedings in the West German Courts to contest his forced membership and the subsidy he did not want.

*... a novel idea for 'mowing' the lawn*

# MIND THAT HORSE!

The British police officer really is a splendid fellow, resourceful and energetic, an equal to every challenge that the variegated course of duty may present to him.

PC John Pritty could hardly believe his eyes in January 1986 when, as he was about to drive onto the M1 at the Edgware Way intersection in North-West London, he saw six frightened horses on the road ahead of him just about to dash out onto Britain's busiest motorway.

What did he do? He brought a touch of the Wild West to London's North West. He stopped his car, rushed round to the boot, took out a length of rope and fashioned it into a lasso. Then with the help of three passing girls who had hastened to his assistance, he triumphantly led the horses back into the field from which they had wandered. Gary Cooper could not have done better.

# CROCODILE TEARS

Crocodiles are not one of my favourite animals, and I shouldn't think I am alone in this. But people take a different view in the Australian state of Queensland.

Shortly before Christmas 1985, Beryl Wruck, a forty-three-year-old storekeeper, waded into a creek in the state's northern tourist area and never came back. Friends were convinced that she had been eaten by a crocodile. The incident prompted Queensland's Environment Minister to propose that all crocodiles in the area should be caught or shot. The plan angered Australian conservationists. 'It is hard to defend creatures that are not cute or cuddly,' said the co-ordinator of the State Conservation Council. 'But they do not deserve to die because they aren't cute.'

In due course, the Queensland Cabinet approved the round-up. A day later, about a mile downstream from where Wruck had disappeared, officials captured a sixteen-foot crocodile with fingernails, toenails and crushed bone in its stomach.

It takes more than that to put off a determined crocodile-lover. Said the chairman of a local tourist organisation, offering sanctuary to any threatened beast: 'We have learned to live with crocks the same way city people live with peak-hour traffic. No-one steps onto a freeway at 5 pm.'

# THE JUDGE WHO LOVED THE GEE-GEES

Mr Justice Hawkins, who died, as Lord Brampton, at the venerable age of ninety in 1907, was one of the most famous and delightfully eccentric judges of the Victorian Age. Not only did he always sit in court with his dog on the chair beside him, but he was notorious for his love of horse-racing.

He was sitting once at the Lincoln Assize Court on the morning of the Lincoln Handicap. At the close of a case, he turned to the jury and said: 'Gentlemen of the jury, it has been brought to my notice that there is an event of some local importance about to take place this afternoon. I should be loath to stand for a moment between you and your participation in the celebration. Any expression of opinion on your part, therefore, will receive my most serious consideration.'

The jury took the hint. After a few moments' deliberation between themselves, the foreman arose and announced that they had 'no expression of opinion to offer.'

'I thank you for your communication, gentlemen,' said the judge. 'The Court is adjourned until eleven o'clock tomorrow morning!'

In another year, it was the Epsom Derby that the judge was particularly anxious to attend. But he was subtle about it. Without revealing his desire, he asked a QC who was in the case before him to come and see him in his private room. He suggested to the QC that it might perhaps improve his case if, on the following morning, he pressed for an adjournment.

A wink was as good as a nudge. The next morning in court the distinguished 'Silk' rose to his feet and put the request. 'I am afraid,' said the judge in reply, 'that except for some good reason, I cannot interfere with the ordinary course of business.'

'Well, m'Lord, the fact is, it is a matter of very personal convenience.'

'Oh well,' said the obliging judge. 'Of course, in that case, I have nothing further to say and the case is adjourned.' Within half an hour his Lordship was on his way to the Derby.

One afternoon, a barrister prosecuting before Mr Justice Hawkins a man accused of stealing a tea cup had, in the middle of his address to the jury, a telegram put into his hand. He broke off, read it – and could not stop himself saying delightedly: 'Silvio's won – and I've won!'

His Lordship was furious. He demanded to know the meaning of it all. The barrister apologised profusely for his conduct and begged forgiveness. Hawkins replied: 'It is most improper, and I trust it will never occur again.'

Prosecuting counsel was about to resume his speech, when the judge interrupted him again: 'Oh, by the way, did the telegram say what was second and third?'

But perhaps my favourite of all the many 'Hanging Hawkins' stories is this one: Soon after he had been promoted to the Bench, he was presiding over a murder trial when prosecuting counsel saw the prisoner in the dock say something to a constable; counsel demanded that what had been said should be disclosed. 'Yes,' said Hawkins, 'I think you may demand that. Constable, inform the Court what passed between you and the prisoner.'

'I ... I would rather not, your Lordship, I was ...'

'Never mind what you would rather not do,' interrupted the judge angrily. 'Inform the Court what the prisoner said.'

'He asked me, your Lordship, who that hoary heathen with the sheepskin was, as he had often seen him at the racecourse.'

Rather like old Hollywood movies, sadly they don't make judges like that any more!

# ARREST THAT BEETLE!

An animal, or even an insect, could never be too large or too small to escape the vengeance of the law.

In 1499, a bear was put on trial in Germany on a charge of terrorising local villages. Defence counsel's plea that his client had the right to be tried by a jury consisting of his fellow bears was rejected. In 1601, a horse that had been taught some curious tricks by his owner was publicly tried at Lisbon, and when found 'guilty of being possessed by the devil', was sentenced to be burned at the stake.

At the other end of the spectrum of size, legal proceedings were instituted in France in 1545, at St Julien de Maurienne, against some beetles that had ravaged the nearby vineyards. A lawyer was assigned to defend them, but the insects suddenly left and the prosecution was discontinued.

Forty-two years later the beetles returned. Perhaps they thought that the old indictment had been forgotten. But if so, they were mistaken. The prosecution was renewed. A judge was named to try them and a lawyer assigned to defend them. The court's decree was that the owners of the vineyard should provide another piece of land, containing ample trees and shrubbery, where the beetles could happily live without troubling the vines. Almost a judgement of Solomon, one might think.

A similar prosecution was instituted against caterpillars in Port-du-Chateau, in the Auvergne, in France, in 1690 when the insects were excommunicated and relegated to an uncultivated spot designated by the court. Perhaps there is a hangover from those days of prosecuting insects in the present bye-law in Brussels which carries a possible penalty of imprisonment for anyone who fails to kill a furry caterpillar, if they have the chance to do so.

*She hid 6,000 bees and a hive under her habit*

# CONTRABAND BEES

Bees are considered to be livestock under the law of Kenya and an import permit is needed to bring them into the country. The reason is that beekeeping is a multi-million pound industry in that African nation, with the country exporting 13,000 metric tons of honey and several thousand tons of bees' wax every year.

Sister Irene, a Greek Orthodox nun, returning to Kenya on a flight from Greece in December 1984, did not worry herself with high finance. She wanted to bring bees into the country to produce candles for the church in Riruta, a suburb of Nairobi. She must have been wearing voluminous clothing, for she hid 6,000 European bees and a hive under her habit while passing through the Customs at Nairobi Airport, and no-one stopped her.

Her misdemeanour was only discovered when she herself took some of the European bees to the Ministry of Agriculture so that they could be compared and mated with local varieties. When she failed to produce an import permit, Ministry officials alerted the police and she was arrested. The church never got its candles, for the bees were all destroyed and the poor Sister was charged with the illegal importation of 'livestock' and faced a maximum fine of £500 or up to five years in prison.

# *FELINE FAVOURITES*

Judge 'Hanging' Hawkins may have loved his dog, but there is no doubt at all that it is cats who really are the spoiled darlings of the law. No destruction order can ever be made against them, however viciously clawed they may be, as is, of course, not the case with dogs. They can, in the eyes of centuries of British judges, scarcely do no wrong.

I literally know of no case, reported in the law books or in my own many years of practice at the Bar, where a cat owner has been made to pay damages in court; and, as for the criminal law, I have discovered only one case (see 'The Cat That Made Legal History') where a cat owner has ended up before magistrates because of his feline friend.

In 1926, when a suburban houseowner with a chicken run in his back garden unsuccessfully sued a neighbour whose cat had slaughtered some of his chickens, Lord Justice Atkin ruled: 'The owner of a cat is not rendered liable by the mere fact that the animal does damage in following a natural propensity of its kind to do damage.' One could not have a *carte blanche* more *blanche* than that!

Cats have been chasing – and killing – birds since the beginning of time; and there is nothing the law (or cat owners) can do about it. The Animals Act of 1971 was supposed, at least in one important respect, to have changed all that. The Act contained a specific clause that all animal owners – including cat owners – were thenceforth to be under a legal duty to take reasonable care to prevent their animals getting out onto the highway and causing an accident.

There was a lot of talk at the time about cat owners under this new law being at last liable for mishaps caused by their pets shooting out onto the road and forcing cars to swerve and bicycles to brake sharply, and suchlike. But it did not happen. How could it? How can you be expected to take 'reasonable care' to prevent your cat getting out onto the road, without turning your house and garden into a feline Fort Knox?

# ANIMAL LIBERATION

Four teenagers who raided a pet shop in London's Shepherds Bush Market with the best of intentions, still found themselves at Marylebone Magistrates' Court, in May 1982, pleading guilty to breaking into the shop and stealing its animals.

'I don't agree with any animals being chained or locked up, so we took leads and dog collars too,' one of them told the Court. 'We were appalled by the way the creatures were being kept. We were just going to look after the animals until we could find decent homes for them, and we took pet food to feed them.' But freedom sadly proved a mixed blessing to the thirty mice who were among the fifty-five animals released from their cages: they were promptly gobbled up by two cats, also freed by the resolute raiders. In the end, the four defendants were conditionally discharged and each ordered to pay £25 compensation and £20 costs.

# *THE CAT THAT MADE LEGAL HISTORY*

Tiddles was a delightful cat, much beloved by his mistress, and when he went missing in late 1979, she was distraught.

Some eighteen months later, her husband, a London eye specialist with a large practice in Marylebone, was absolutely thrilled one day to see Tiddles quietly snoring on the bonnet of a car parked in a Soho street. Unfortunately, Tiddles appears not to have been so pleased to see him. As the doctor picked up the long lost tabby, Tiddles lashed out with his claws and scratched the bodywork of the car on which he had been snoozing; thirty-one scratches, to be precise. A passing policewoman, zealous in enforcement of the law, witnessed the extraordinary scene, and promptly arrested the bewildered doctor for criminal damage.

'It is a somewhat bizarre and strange matter, to say the least,' said the prosecuting lawyer at Marlborough Street Magistrates' Court in July 1981. 'I should make it quite clear that the damage had actually been occasioned by the cat. But at the same time, the prosecution makes it clear that the cat is the innocent agent of the defendant, and the defendant is answerable as principal.'

So the unfortunate doctor, who had all along denied the charge, was conditionally discharged for six months and ordered to pay £25 legal costs, plus £20.70 compensation to the car's owner. But at least he got Tiddles back.

# A SHAGGY HORSE STORY

In November 1972, a stable owner looked his new horse in the mouth and became suspicious that the animal was longer in the tooth than had been stated in the sale catalogue at Steyning Market where he had bought him. So he told the magistrates at Steyning Magistrates' Court.

The horse dealer had claimed that the horse, a black gelding called Tarmac, was seven years old, but a veterinary surgeon backed up the buyer's suspicions with the confident assertion that the animal was in fact 'at least ten'. The defending lawyer put up a good fight. 'Despite all the stories afoot about wicked horse dealers,' he told the Bench, 'I would ask you to think that there is no villainy here at all.'

But their Worships were not so sure. They fined the dealer £50 for giving a 'false trade description' contrary to the Trade Descriptions Act of 1968. They were, however, almost Solomon-like in their deliberations. For the dealer also faced a second charge in which it was alleged that his further claim that the horse was a 'winner of show jumping at Hickstead' was false. Can you be 'a winner' if you are not *the* winner?

The magistrates said 'Yes', and threw out the charge. For, although Tarmac had never come first in an equestrian event, he had won a £1 prize for coming tenth in a Foxhunter Novice Event at the famous Hickstead grounds. That was enough to justify the dealer's second claim.

# SPECIAL CONSTABLES

It was the parrot which squawked when its owner's home in Baytown, Texas, was burgled. The intruders must have called out to each other while ransacking the house because the owner returned to find his parrot repeating two names: Robert and Ronnie. The local police knew two burglars with those names who worked as a team, and they were soon behind bars – thanks to the bird who gave the word.

But the animals more regularly employed in law enforcement are horses and dogs. In 1984 alone the horses of the Metropolitan Police Mounted Division in London consumed an estimated 194 tonnes of oats, 64 tonnes of bran, 357 tonnes of hay, 422 tonnes of straw, 64 tonnes of chaff and 32 tonnes of linseed. The bill for all this, and for removing manure from police stables, was £155,000.

Police horses are also, of course, a regular feature of American crime detection. However, not every incident is a happy one. In 1985 a man in Houston, Texas, whose car was damaged by a police horse was told that the City would not foot his $600 bill for repairs – because the animal was not a 'motorised vehicle'.

In London, police and dogs have co-operated in the fight against crime for nearly 100 years. In 1888 bloodhounds were brought into the 'Jack the Ripper' case as public hysteria about the famous murders mounted; but the experiment ended when the then Commissioner, Sir Charles Warren, was bitten by one of them.

In 1914, at the start of World War I, 172 police constables were given permission to take their own dogs on duty, though it was more for company than for any practical use. In 1938 two dogs – both labradors – were

introduced into the London Metropolitan Police on an experimental basis, but the outbreak of World War II put paid to that.

It was only in 1946 that 'the Met' finally decided to try dogs officially and on a permanent basis. Six labradors were trained and were so successful that today there are 312 dogs operational with the force – all of them German Shepherds (or alsatians as some people call them), except for one labrador, one Weimaraner and one Bouvier des Flanders. Although there is no official restriction on the breed of dog the police use, the German Shepherd is the clear favourite. Anyone who has faced one in anger will know the reason why.

But mistakes can happen even with the best trained police dog. In 1985 there were two unfortunate incidents. In Thetford in Norfolk, a police dog got the wrong man when it was called to break up a fight in a pub car park. Instead of tackling the half-dozen men involved in the brawl, it bit a policeman! 'Alas, when arms and legs are flying, a dog just goes for the nearest one,' said a colleague – who was not bitten.

Similarly, it was perhaps not entirely the dog's fault when another police hound urinated on the carpets and pinned a lodger to a wall during a drugs raid on a house in Falmouth, Cornwall. It didn't help matters either that it was the wrong house.

# BUNNY LAW

It is perhaps difficult to imagine circumstances in which a rabbit could cause a human being to end up in court, but it has happened on at least two occasions in Britain within recent years.

The first case was in July 1980, when a resident of Swindon was fined £20 with £28.50 costs by the local magistrates for abandoning his pet rabbit in a park, and thereby causing it unnecessary suffering. One might have thought that the rabbit would easily have adapted to what was, at least, its ancestors' natural habitat; but the Bench took a stern view of the case, also fining the man's wife £10 for 'permitting' the offence. What happened to the rabbit? The RSPCA found it a new home – presumably not in a park.

The other rabbit case was rather more substantial:

A middle-aged woman antiques dealer from Woburn tried to flag down an approaching car, when she saw a rabbit trying to cross a busy local road. Unfortunately, the driver did not stop his car in time and, although the rabbit got away scot-free, the do-gooding lady suffered extensive leg injuries, resulting in severe scarring.

In November 1982, in the High Court in London, Mr Justice Kenneth Brown awarded the woman £5,000 damages, although he described her valiant rescue as 'absolute folly'. In fact she would have got £7,500 damages if the judge had not reduced her claim by one-third because he took the view that she was, in that proportion, to blame for the accident herself since she had not exercised reasonable care for her own safety – what the law calls 'contributory negligence'.

The woman was undeterred and was quoted afterwards as saying: 'I might be stupid but I'd probably do the same thing again.' There was no comment from the rabbit.

# SOMETHING FISHY

In January 1983, the Ministry of Agriculture, Fisheries and Food startled the readers of the *Daily Telegraph* by using that distinguished newspaper to inform the general public that anyone releasing bitterling, pumpkinseed, wels or zander into the wild in England and Wales might be committing an offence. What on earth were these improbable-sounding creatures? They were, in fact, varieties of fish which had become established in the wild and had been listed in the Ninth Schedule to the Wild Life and Countryside Act of 1981, that had recently come into effect. The pumpkinseed is also known as the sun-fish or pond-perch, while the wels's alias is the European catfish. The Ninth Schedule also referred to the large-mouthed black bass and the rock bass.

Releasing any of these species, or any 'other fish or shellfish not ordinarily resident in Great Britain', or their eggs, whether deliberately or unintentionally, into the wild in England and Wales was an offence, the Ministry warned. Unless that is, the release had been authorised by an individual licence.

The Ministry also helpfully added that types of fish which *could* be released into the wild in England and Wales included rainbow trout, Japanese or Pacific oysters and Portuguese oysters, or any eggs of those species. Into which part of England or Wales it was likely that a Portuguese oyster might be usefully released, the Ministry did not condescend to say.

Two young men who appeared before the Barnsley magistrates in August 1981 were not concerned with such exotic fish as were to be named in the Agriculture Ministry's handout. Their problem was the much humbler goldfish.

The men had heard that shops were charging £6 each for these shimmering little fishes, so they went on a night-time poaching expedition to the well-stocked pond at a local school in order to steal some. They were not very competent villains. They made so much noise that a neighbour called the police and they were caught, not only red-handed but empty-handed. Charged with attempting to steal the school's supply of goldfish and breaking into a potting shed, they were fined £80 each. The Chairman of the Bench told them: 'Going out into the night to steal goldfish is absolutely ridiculous. One attributes this to children rather than grown men.'

*Unusual precautions were required ...*

# ANTI-THEFT DEVICE

In December 1981, the Sri Lankan Festival at the Commonwealth Institute in London had a somewhat exceptional security officer on duty.

Unusual precautions were required to protect a most unusual collection of jewellery, including the third largest star sapphire in the world. So the authorities hit upon the novel idea of placing a highly poisonous cobra in the showcase alongside the gem. 'I do not know whether it is better than the modern electronic security systems. We have those as well,' explained the First Secretary to the Sri Lankan High Commission, 'but it is very venomous and should stop anyone trying to steal the gem.'

The device certainly succeeded. No attempts whatsoever were made to try and remove the sapphire. But was the law not broken by having the cobra on duty? Not at all. The cobra came from a private collection in London and a keeper was on hand to feed it and check its condition. As the RSPCA explained: 'Providing the cobra is being kept in much the same conditions as it would be at a private zoo, and it is being fed and watered, I don't think we would have anything against it.' And neither would the Dangerous Wild Animals Act of 1976.

# THE ONE-EYED COW

A one-eyed cow named Rosemary the Third, said to be bad-tempered, set a legal problem for Mr Justice Watkins in the High Court in London, in May 1979.

A herdsman was suing Rosemary's owners, and his ex-employers, for their alleged failure to operate a safe system of work. His counsel explained to the judge that Rosemary was one of a 100-strong milking herd at a farm near Hailsham in Sussex. Although she was a good milk producer, she was bad-tempered, aggressive and liable to kick. Other herdsmen were not prepared to handle or milk her, so the bulk of this work fell upon his client.

On the day of the accident, the herdsman was spraying Rosemary with de-lousing powder when she kicked his left knee, crushing it against an iron bar. It was a bad accident. The man took pride in his job and felt he could not do his work properly any more, so a year later he left. He tried his hand at labouring, selling insurance and later as an agricultural salesman. But he was never happy and gave up that last job two months before the court case. He now intended to sign up with a Government Re-training Course.

Did Rosemary's owners have to pay for their one-eyed cow's high kick? 'No,' ruled the judge, at the end of a three-day hearing. Mr Justice Watkins proved himself extremely understanding of the vagaries of cows. He said that poor Rosemary was probably more nervous than the rest of the herd because of her partial blindness. He rejected the herdsman's claim, and accepted the farm owners' contention that the accident was all his own fault.

Even one-eyed cows have rights under the beneficent rules of English law.

# DUCKS AND DRAKES

Can a man have sexual intercourse with a duck? The question was raised in the case, beloved of all law students, that is enshrined forever in the 1889 Volume of the 'Queen's Bench Division' Law Reports under the name of *Regina v Brown*.

Lord Coleridge, the Lord Chief Justice, had dealt with a case on Assize in Essex, in which a young man standing before him had been indicted with 'attempting to commit unnatural offences with domestic fowls'. The Report tells us that the depositions showed 'that in all probability the offence had been habitual with him, and had resulted in the death of several of the birds, and serious injury to several others, who were found torn and bleeding apparently from the effects of the attempted penetration.'

The would-be duck-lover tried to save everyone the trouble of deciding whether in law he could be guilty of the offence by confessing and insisting on pleading guilty. The shocked Lord Chief Justice, his heart unmelted by the man's own admission of error, sentenced him to twelve months' imprisonment with hard labour. But afterwards Lord Coleridge had his doubts: could you attempt the impossible? And was a duck an 'animal' within the meaning of the then current Victorian statute for the protection of animals? He referred the case to the Court for Crown Cases Reserved in London, where on 2 November 1889 the President of that court pronounced judgement. He was the same Lord Coleridge, the Lord Chief Justice!

In the event, his Lordship felt able to uphold his own ruling. He rejected his subsequent doubts that a duck was not 'an animal' within the meaning of the Victorian Act, and further held that it was no defence to attempting a crime to say that it was impossible to complete. He went further, saying: 'I should suppose it is obvious that the offence could be committed by the boy' – for reasons which the Report does not deign to tell us. Perhaps the learned Lord Chief Justice knew more about the mysterious ways of duck-lovers than he was prepared to say in open court.